CONTENTS

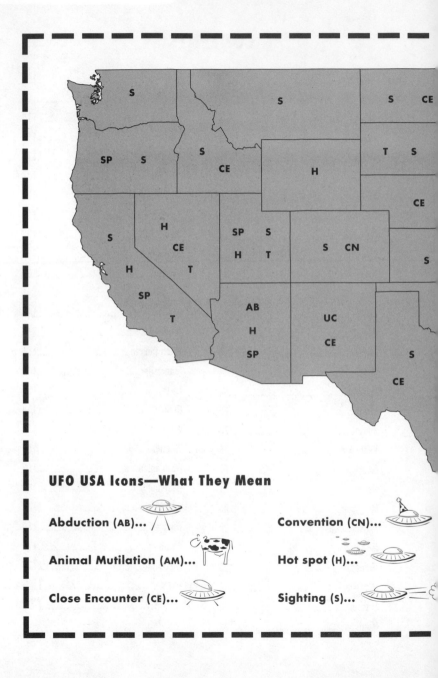

UFO USA Icons—What They Mean

Abduction (AB)...

Animal Mutilation (AM)...

Close Encounter (CE)...

Convention (CN)...

Hot spot (H)...

Sighting (S)...

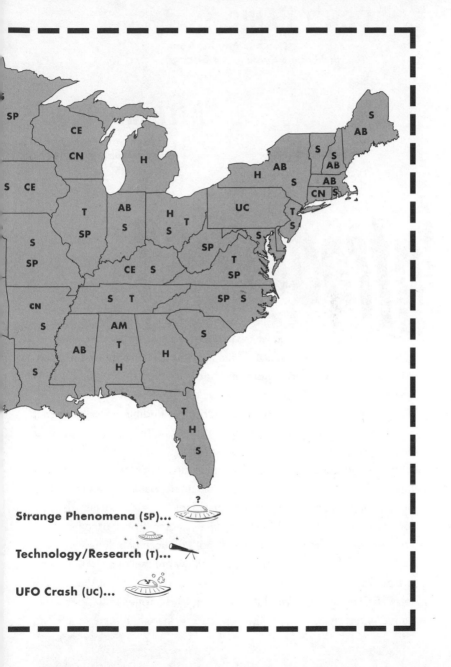

Strange Phenomena (SP)...

Technology/Research (T)...

UFO Crash (UC)...

"DON'T PANIC."

Douglas Adams, from
The Hitchhiker's Guide to the Galaxy

"KEEP MOVING."

Hunter S. Thompson, from
Fear and Loathing in Las Vegas

Introduction

If, as they say, "The truth is out there"—then where the heck is it?

Is there really extraterrestrial life, or are there just a lot of people in the world with big imaginations and bad eyesight? This is the $64,000 question that UFO hunters and alien seekers, both serious and amateur, have been attempting to answer for years. But finding the truth, when it comes to UFO hunting, is like attaching banana peels to your feet and heading out onto the ice—very slippery stuff.

But a lot of people, short and tall, rich and poor, black and white, city folks and country folks, physicists and plumbers, believe that somewhere out there in the vast universe there is intelligent life—and that they drop by for a visit every now and then. Many other people (from that same broad cross-section of human existence) say that's a bunch of baloney.

Serious ufologists will tell you that ninety percent of all UFO reports are proven to have nothing to do with extraterrestrial life. (After all, the term *UFO* means only what it stands for, and implies nothing more—*Unidentified Flying Object*.) But what about the other ten percent? The other ten percent can't be explained by any known phenomenon, and it's why ufologists bother looking. It's why they work a day job and volunteer to go sniffing around strange places, eating greasy food from Styrofoam containers in their cars, tracking down elusive clues at night and on weekends. And when you think about the fact that most ufologists believe that only a small portion of UFO sightings and close encounters are actually reported, this means that the unexplained ten percent may be a little bit bigger after all.

So where exactly is this ten percent, and how can you get in on the action? Well "the truth" may be out there in Georgia, Florida, New York, Puerto Rico, or even in your own neighborhood, and this book will help you go find it for yourself. With it you can go to many of the major extraterrestrial points of interest in the United States and its territories—the sites of historical UFO incidents, alleged military cover-ups, frightening abduction cases, and UFO "hot spots," as well as museums, observatories, and other roadside attractions.

There is no guarantee that in using this book you will see a UFO. You may see what you think is a UFO—only to discover later that it was a helicopter or a meteor or a weather balloon. And that's an important thing to keep in mind—just because something is called a UFO, doesn't mean an alien is behind its wheel. UFO means Unidentified Flying Object. It means you have seen something and don't know what it was. Another thing to keep in mind is that hard science has still not permeated to the core of the UFO world—though many people are trying to marry the two. Many

Factoid: According to an Associated Press poll, sixty percent of all Americans think there is intelligent life on other planets. Forty-seven percent of all Americans believe these visitors are more intelligent than we are. Eighty-six percent believe our galactic neighbors are friendly.

of the reports of close encounters you will read about here cannot be proven—and what really stinks is that they often lead to more questions.

THE TWO COMMON TYPES OF UFOs:
   Nocturnal lights—The most commonly reported type of UFO. They come in all shapes and sizes. Some are small spots of light; some are larger and look like balls. They often move in strange and unpredictable patterns. (See in particular Marfa, Texas, or Joplin, Missouri.)
   Crafts—The most common types of crafts are shaped like saucers, boomerangs, diamonds, cigars, or triangles. They often have bright lights, often red or white. Other times they are multicolored. At times, they are reported to emit beams or shafts of light. Some UFOs move at incredible speeds, others hover or move slowly through the sky.

This is why the credibility of a witness becomes a crucial part of a ufologist's investigation. In doing research of this kind, you are often at the mercy of completely anecdotal evidence. What we have attempted to do is to cull from a mountain of reliable literature the most significant, historical, and reliable UFO cases, with the help of consulting editor and Ufologist Antonio Huneeus (MUFON's international coordinator and author of hundreds of articles on UFOs). Many of the cases in this book are still anecdotal in nature, but have lots of independent witnesses or other evidence to back it up.

Within this book, you will also find information to aid you in your personal UFO tour of the United States, whether you're simply interested in UFO watching, or you actually want a close encounter of a different kind. *UFO USA* is a crash course in ufology—its language, its key players, its history, its organizations. If you're interested in learning more about the study of UFOs (or in contacting research organizations to find out the most up-to-date UFO incidents), you will find tons of terrific resources to help you do that too.

So, best of luck on your UFO travels. Have a blast, and don't forget to look up. May the force be with you and may the force be a friendly one.

Heading Out on the Road: What You Need to Do, Take, and Know

....

Be prepared—it's a good motto on any planet, and this brief chapter will give you the essential tips and information you need before you are ready to begin your UFO trek. From how to begin your journey to what to take on a skywatch, it's all below.

UFO Watching: What You Need

Mechanical stopwatch

Ruler

Binoculars or telescope

Flashlight

Pencil and paper

Video or still camera and a tripod

Increasing Your Chances of Seeing a UFO:

In the United States, UFOs are sighted in each state with the greatest number of reports coming from the Northeast and the Southwest. Pine Bush, New York; La Grange, Georgia; Phoenix, Arizona; Colorado's San Luis Valley; and Gulf Breeze, Florida, are the United States' most consistently active UFO hot spots.

Tips to Keep in Mind:

1. Go to an area known for repeated UFO activity. UFO activity is not like lightning. It tends to strike the same areas again and again.

2. Sightings generally occur in rural areas, in small towns, over water, and near military installations.

3. According to the Center for UFO Studies (CUFOS), one of the nation's premier ufology groups, most sightings occur around 9:00 P.M. with a secondary peak at about 3:00 A.M. UFO reports are evenly distributed throughout the week, with peak periods of reports coming

during the summer months, especially July. Some ufologists disagree and believe that you are more likely to see a UFO on Wednesday night and less likely on Friday and Saturday nights.

UFO Watching Tips:

1. Never go alone. The more witnesses to a sighting, the more seriously your report will be taken.
2. Stay calm. If you freak out or become excited, you're likely to forget to notice important details.
3. Know some basic astronomy. The more educated you are as to the position and behavior of stars and meteors, the less likely you will be to mistake a UFO for an IFO (Identifiable Flying Object) and then feel like a dope.
4. Be patient and persistent. Remember, there are folks who have been researching and investigating UFOs for years who have never seen one in the skies.
5. Wear sneakers. You just never know when you'll have to make a run for it.

What to Do If You See a UFO:

In order to provide the most accurate and helpful information to investigators, Mark Cashman of the Connecticut chapter of the Mutual UFO Network (MUFON), one of the best-known national UFO investigative groups, offers this technical advice for observing:

1. Accurately record the time at the start of the observation, the time of any direction change, and the time of the end of the sighting. If possible, use a mechanical stopwatch, since close proximity (within five hundred feet) of a UFO can prevent electronic instruments from functioning.
2. Hold up a ruler to the object at arm's length and measure the size of the object according to that ruler. Then, afterward, measure the length of your arm. These items, in conjunction with other data, may allow

IFOs THAT ARE MOST COMMONLY MISTAKEN FOR UFOs:
Airplanes
Atmospheric disturbances
Ball lightning
Blimps
Meteors
Naturally occurring light phenomena
Planets
Satellites
Stars
Unconventional or secret military aircraft
Weather balloons

determination of the size of the observed object. If the object is observed in several positions, it should be measured at each position, especially if there is an apparent size change.

3. Mark a position on the ground at the start of the observation. Draw a line on the ground in the direction of the object when first seen, for each direction change, and when last seen. Use chalk if possible, and number the lines in sequence. If two observers separated by some distance (preferably at least one hundred feet, ideally more than five hundred feet) do this, it is possible to obtain a triangulation to the object, which will allow you to determine the object's distance, and, in conjunction with the apparent size of the object, this can be used to determine an estimated size for the object. Note that observers cannot reliably estimate distances or sizes of unknown objects beyond five hundred feet; triangulation is the only reliable method at any distance. If an observer is driving, it is also possible to obtain a triangulation if they can line up the position of the UFO at two positions about five hundred feet apart, hopefully within a short time interval. Identifying proximity of the object in regard to a horizon landmark and the stopping point of the car in regard to a ground landmark for each position is helpful.

UFO Hunter's Tip: No Trespassing!

An important thing to remember so we don't get yelled at: Some of the places mentioned in this book are located on private property, so we were obliged to leave out exact addresses. But the fact is that people are often willing to share their experiences with others who are polite, respectful, and interested. It's pretty easy to find out where UFO-related things happened, especially in small towns. If you ask, you might even be allowed to investigate or skywatch on private property. But ask! Don't climb other people's fences or trample on public or private gardens either.

Military installations are heavily guarded. You don't want to mess with these people. Stay off government land if you're not authorized to be there. There is, however, no law that prevents you from skywatching from nearby military installations and landing strips. The point is, go where the action is but don't get arrested or place yourself in physical danger. Use your common sense if you have it.

4. If the object can be demonstrated to have been hovering at one physical location and to have gone from a hover to pass demonstrably over another location, the time taken to do that can be used to determine acceleration. Accurate time estimates of that period are essential. Note that this is generally only useful in the case of close encounters, because of the difficulty in determining position or even whether or not the object is actually hovering in more distant sightings.

5. Neither video nor conventional film camera images carry much weight by themselves. Video images are useful for recording the position and direction changes of an object, but only when the camera is on a stable tripod and only when the direction of the camera throughout the sighting has been recorded. The same is true for still cameras. In both cases, it is essential that reference information in the form of treeline, buildings, etc. appear consistently in the images along with the object. Researchers are naturally cautious about video and still photos, since these are hoaxed very frequently.

6. The sighting should be reported to the National UFO Reporting Center as soon as possible, so that the sighting can be filtered and transmitted to the local level if deemed valid as soon as possible. (See page 176 for resource information on the NUFORC.) Essential information can be lost or distorted in the witness memory the longer the sighting is not investigated, and the records of air traffic and other possible IFO sources are also harder to obtain over time.

7. Observers should note that the NUFORC, MUFON, and CUFOS associates who investigate sightings are volunteers with limited time and resources, and that reports of point source lights or distant triangular objects, which are likely to be aircraft, stars, planets, satellites, or other misinterpreted phenomena are unlikely to be investigated. And, obviously, hoaxes are to be discouraged. So don't cry alien!

UFO USA: STATE-BY-STATE

Alabama
....

EASTERN ALABAMA

Head one hundred miles south of Birmingham toward the Georgia border and you will find yourself smack dab in the middle of what many people consider prime UFO country! While the nearby area of La Grange, Georgia (see page 53) is better known for its alleged UFO activity, this section of Alabama shares most of the same sightings and incidents (folks here are just quieter about it—there's the major difference between Alabama and Georgia, says local MUFON director, Jim Thompson).

The Story:

About forty miles closer to the Georgia state line (and about eighty-five miles east of Montgomery) is the small town of **Valley, Alabama.** In 1996, a local farmer took six pictures of an alleged UFO that caused a stir when it was reported by TV–33 in LaGrange, Georgia. *The Atlanta Journal and Constitution* also ran a story of the reported Valley UFO flap. The pictures reveal an acorn-shaped object in the sky. The authenticity of the photos has been hotly debated. But one thing is for sure—this area of Alabama is no stranger to alleged reports of UFO activity.

UFO Watching:

MUFON Director Thompson recommends sky-viewing near Valley on **West Point Lake** (which straddles Georgia and Alabama). There have been numerous sightings here. Camping facilities and cabins are available but only in the spring and summer so call first—706-645-2937. From Valley, take Highway 29 east toward West Point, Georgia. You will cross over the state line and then back into Alabama. This takes you right into the park.

Or, Thompson says to head to **Bald Rock** near Wadley in Randolph County. Bald Rock is a huge boulder of exposed granite, which, he says, may be a draw for UFOs. (Perhaps they use it on their saucer dashboards?) There is a church that conducts sunrise services there, so Sunday is not the best time to visit unless you have a suit handy. To get there, travel out of Wadley (about an hour from Valley) on Route 77 north about four miles. When you see an abandoned store on your right, turn left and follow the dirt road to the bridge. Park around the bridge and walk from there, you'll see the cross the church has erected on the rock. If you get lost any local can direct you and you can stop in at the county courthouse for directions as well.

For More Information:

Greater Valley Chamber of Commerce, 334-642-1411.
Randolph County Chamber of Commerce, 334-863-6612.

HUNTSVILLE

If you've dreamed of meeting aliens on their turf or of taking a blast into the "final frontier," Huntsville is the place to go. Located on the foothills of the Appalachians, Huntsville is the space capital of the United States and probably the most cosmopolitan of all of Alabama's cities. But don't worry, residents swear that you will still get the small-town hospitality Alabama is famous for.

In 1950, Senator John Sparkman (a resident of Huntsville) brought a team of German rocket scientists to Redstone Arsenal to develop rockets for the U.S. Army. Under the leadership of Wernher von Braun, the team went on to develop the rocket which orbited America's first satellite. This

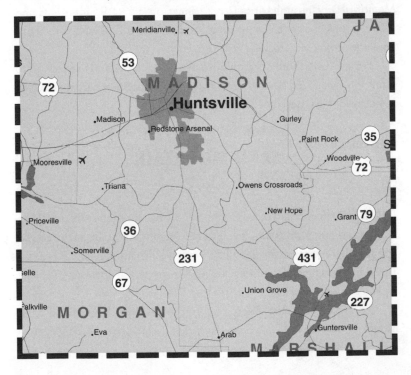

rocket technology eventually transported the first astronauts to the Moon.

The legacy of the space program has a huge presence in Huntsville thanks to the **U.S. Space and Rocket Center**—the world's largest space attraction. But this isn't a place where you just walk around and see old rockets in glass cases. You can feel simulated weightlessness, feel the G forces of a launch aboard the "Space Shot," watch movies shot by astronauts in space, tour the NASA-Marshall Space Flight Center, and train in the "Space Academy." New attractions include the MIR core module now on display.

The Site:

The U.S. Space and Rocket Center (One Tranquility Base, Huntsville, AL 35807) is open daily from 9 to 5, September through May; and 9 to 6, Memorial Day through Labor Day. Admission is $14.95 for adults and $10.95 for kids. For more information call 256-837-3400. Gift shop, cafeteria, coffee bar, picnic area.

From Birmingham or Nashville take 65 to I5-65 and use Exit 15 to reach the center. You have to make reservations for **Space Camp,** which is mostly for kids, but some adults are tolerated.

SAND MOUNTAIN

Tucked into the northern corner of the state, between Huntsville and Chattanooga, is Sand Mountain. If you're not color-blind, go in the fall so you can watch the leaves turning colors when you're not looking at the sky. This is the best time of year to visit this sweeping tree-covered vista with wide rivers and cool lakes.

Just watch your step. Because if you're going to skywatch on Sand Mountain, you may run into a cow or two that's missing a few key parts—usually in the places that make us humans cringe.

The Story:

If you read UFO magazines, newsletters, or the newsgroups, you quickly discover that many people believe that because cattle mutilations are allegedly accompanied by UFO sightings, there's a connection between the two. After all, the argument goes, who else but aliens (we hope) would want the reproductive parts of cattle? Often, it appears that there is a lack of tangible physical evidence at these mutilation sites, making a reasonable explanation for the mutilations even harder to come by. Often there are no tire tracks, no footprints, and no witnesses—zilch—just some upset cattle owners. Some people think, though it's never been proven, that the military may be performing secret tests on the cattle. Others think that the air force has been collaborating with the aliens, and that joint experimentation is taking place. Others say, no way can the government keep anything secret. This is one of those major head-scratchers.

One community located on Sand Mountain—**Fyffe**—is a particularly unfriendly place to be if you are a cow. According to an April 1993 press release issued by the city of Fyffe, mutilated cattle began appearing here and in other areas of De Kalb County in October of 1993. But the local newspaper, the *Weekly Post,* began reporting sightings of strange crafts in the area's skies way back in 1989. There were so many sightings of UFOs that the Alabama State Senate declared it the "UFO capital of Alabama." There is supposedly a major UFO sighting in DeKalb County every ten to twelve years, with a few minor sightings in between. Residents have reported seeing everything from small cigar-shaped crafts to banana-shaped crafts the size of football fields hovering overhead—although no marching band was seen or heard.

A word of advice: When you visit Fyffe, avoid leather apparel.

UFO Watching:

Due to the elevation, skywatching is good anywhere around town and in the county in general. However, there are no camping facilities or state parks on Sand Mountain. For skywatching, head to **Lookout Moun-**

tain, which is the opposite mountain range about a half an hour away by car. From Fyffe, pick up Highway 75 heading toward Rainsville, once you hit this town make a right onto Route 35—this will take you to Lookout Mountain, which has the highest elevation in the county. You can camp at

Filmmaker Linda Howe won an Academy Award (1989) for her documentary, A Strange Harvest, on the Alabama cattle mutilations. (We think it should have been called Close Encounters of the Herd Kind.)

DeSoto State Park, which is on the mountain above Fort Payne. The park is right off Route 35; it's a popular tourist spot so there are lots of signs for the directionally impaired. For more information about camping and lodging facilities in the park, call 800-568-8840.

For More Information:
DeKalb County Tourist Association, 256-845-3957.

Alaska
·············
ANCHORAGE

Anchorage is the place to go if you want to go dogsledding in the morning and skywatching at night. The Northern Lights are really awesome here. Not surprisingly, it was here that one of the most famous UFO sightings was reported. Even the FAA's own reports, which were released to the public, say something unusual was in Alaska's sky on November 17, 1986.

The Story:
According to the FAA report and dozens of other accounts, a Japan Airlines plane was near the end of its Iceland-to-Anchorage leg when its flight

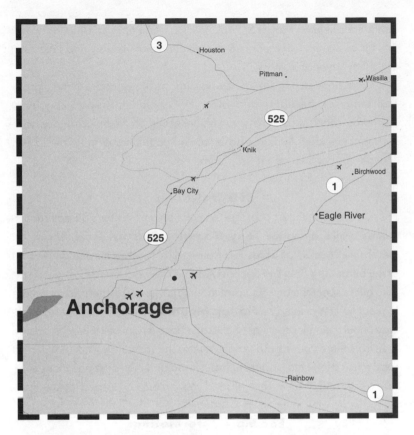

crew saw three unidentified objects. According to Captain Kenju Terauchi, a veteran flyer, the objects appeared to be an immense mothership towing two smaller objects. "It was a very big one, two times bigger than an aircraft carrier." With FAA permission, he began tailing the objects. He reported that the objects moved quickly and stopped suddenly. At one point, the light from the large object was so bright that the crew could feel heat on their faces. After several minutes the UFO vanished.

Both the FAA and the U.S. Air Force initially admitted that the UFO had appeared on their radar. Later, official statements became increasingly vague. But as the *Anchorage Daily News* reported, at a press conference held on March 5, Paul Steucke, FAA Regional Director stated: "As far as we know, the whole crew are people of integrity and did report what they saw accurately."

One skywatcher (in a newsgroup posting) offered the theory that many of the lights and other UFOs that get reported around Anchorage each year are due to light reflecting off the mountains or activity from Elmendorf Air Force Base located on the northern tip of the city. Maybe . . . but then again . . . maybe not.

UFO Watching:

For skywatching, the Anchorage Convention and Visitor's Bureau recommends a hike along the **Tony Knowles Coastal Trail.** This is an eleven-mile coastal trail accessible from several points within the city. To start at the beginning, head to Second Avenue between F and G Streets. This hike offers spectacular water and mountain views. The nearest mountain lookout point is located on **Flattop Mountain.** You take Seaward Highway about four miles south of Anchorage. Take a right on Hillside Road and then from there you will make a right into Chugach State Park. At the next road make a left onto Upper Huffman Road and then after one more mile, take a right on Toilsome. This will lead you to a parking lot and lookout spot.

For More Information:
Anchorage Convention and Visitors Bureau, 907-276-4118.

GAKONA

Let's suppose that aliens attacked us. What would we do? How would we defend ourselves against hostile Extraterrestrial Biological Entities (EBEs) with superior technology? Head to Gakona, Alaska, home of the controversial **HAARP project** and maybe you'll find the answer.

Some say the answer—or the beginning of a new environmental problem—is HAARP, the High-frequency Active Auroral Research Program. This is one subject that has captured the hearts and minds of conspiracy theorists and tech-heads alike.

The Story:

According to Dr. Nick Begich and Jeane Manning, authors of *Angels Don't Play This HAARP: Advances in Tesla Technology,* the United States Navy and Air Force have joined with the University of Alaska, Fairbanks, to build what many believe is a prototype for a ground-based "Star Wars" weapon system located in a remote area of Alaska. Opponents say it's dangerous to the earth's environment because it will eventually heat the upper atmosphere—something like putting toast in a toaster on high.

There isn't a simple explanation for exactly what HAARP is. Ostensibly, HAARP is dedicated to the study of the Earth's ionosphere, the electrically charged belt surrounding our planet's upper atmosphere. Bottom line, nontechnical explanation: it will zap the upper atmosphere with a focused and steerable electromagnetic beam. Electromagnetic waves will then bounce back onto earth and penetrate everything (hence, the toast effect).

According to the navy's official fact sheet on HAARP, it is eventually going to be (phases are still in construction and development) a major arctic facility for upper atmospheric and solar-terrestrial research. It's totally unclassified and its purpose is advanced and improved communication capability. They also maintain that the Alaskan site was required since Alaska is the only state that gives a very wide variety of ionospheric conditions to study. Also, the scientific observation instruments require a quiet electromagnetic location. Such quiet locations are only found away from cities and built-up areas.

When it is completed, the HAARP antenna array will consist of 180 antennas on a total land area of about thirty-three acres.

The Site:

The HAARP research facility is located near mile 11 on the Tok highway, near the village of Gakona in south-central Alaska. Individual tours are not given because of staff limitations. They are working on constructing a visitor's center, but until it's completed (projected for 1999), you must schedule a tour in advance if you have a group of people sincerely interested in learning about this research. The facility is open to the public during their annual open house in August (it's not a fixed date, so you need to check with them). That's when many visitors go and they have experts on hand to explain all the technicalities in lay terms (so people like us can get it). You must submit requests for tours several weeks in advance. You cannot do this by telephone (they do not yet have the staff to deal with questions from the public), so you must do it via snail or e-mail:

Office of Public Affairs Air Force Research Laboratory,
3550 Aberdeen Ave S.E., Kirtland AFB NM 87117-5776,
askhaarp@itd.nrl.navy.mil

Arizona
• • • • • • • • • • • • •
HEBER

Beautiful and tranquil: this is how you would describe the tiny community of Heber, located right in the heart of the Apache-Sitgreaves National Forest. Unless, of course, you were abducted by aliens there.

The Story:

On November 5, 1975 it allegedly happened to **Travis Walton,** and it remains one of the most infamous UFO abduction stories of all time. The case was made famous by the movie, *Fire in the Sky.* According to accounts described in several UFO reference encyclopedias, including the highly regarded *The UFO Book* by UFO researcher Jerome Clark, this is what happened:

Walton and six other forestry workers were heading home in a small truck when they supposedly saw a glowing object shaped like two pie pans hovering above a clearing. Walton left the truck to investigate. To the horror of his coworkers he was allegedly struck with a blue and green

---

THE ABDUCTION TEST
 Think you might have been abducted? Answer the following questions to find out if it's a possibility:
 • **Have you ever experienced "missing" or "lost" time?**
 • **Have you ever had a dream in which you were paralyzed in bed while another being watched you or examined you?**
 • **Do you have any unusual scars or marks with no possible explanation for how you received them?**
 • **Have you ever seen balls, flashes, or beams of light?**
 • **Have you ever awakened from sleep to find yourself in a location other than the one you went to sleep in?**
 • **Do you have a strong reaction to pictures of aliens?**
 • **Do you have recurring memories or dreams of flying through the air or passing through a solid object, like a wall or closed window?**
 • **Do you have strong phobias and an eerie feeling of being watched?**
 • **Do you feel like you "have a mission" to complete?**
 • **Are you tormented by images of needles or other medical implements?**
 • **Are you prone to nose bleeds?**
 • **Do you consider yourself to have psychic abilities?**
 If you answered "yes" to at least three of the above questions, you may have been abducted. Turn to page 176 for resources on how to get help.

---

beam of light from the craft. They reported watching as the light picked Walton up and threw him back on the ground. The driver was frightened and sped away. When they returned minutes later, Walton had seemingly vanished. A police investigation and a massive search followed. Some thought that the men had murdered Walton and were using the UFO story as a cover. They took lie-detector tests and passed.

Five days later, a few miles outside of Heber, Travis Walton was found. He claims that aliens, about five feet in height with domed heads and large creepy eyes, performed experiments on him. He claimed to have seen other, apparently more humanoid, creatures who led him around but would not speak to him. Walton says that he could see stars around the exterior of the craft.

The Site:

To get to the general vicinity of the abduction area, take **Trail #165 in Apache-Sitgreaves National Forest.** Follow State Highway 260 three miles west, then north of the Lakeside Ranger Station. After passing Camp Tatiyee, look for the Mongollon Rim Trail sign. A good parking lot is available. Follow the signs.

If you visit this beautiful national forest located on the Mongollon Rim at sixty-five hundred feet, you'll have plenty of time to contemplate the Walton abduction while enjoying a host of outdoor activities. There are dozens of hiking and cross-country skiing trails, scenic vistas, fishing lakes, and camping areas. Don't forget to write.

For More Information:

Heber Chamber of Commerce, 520-535-4406.

PHOENIX

If you go to Phoenix and wonder why a lot of people are walking and looking up at the same time, it's because this area has become a UFO flap area (an area of allegedly ongoing UFO activity) that has kept residents abuzz since March 13, 1997. That was the night when the skies over Arizona were suddenly filled with glowing orange orbs and triangles—and this town hasn't been the same since.

The Story:

Just about every local newspaper reported the sightings and subsequent investigations. In June 1997, *USA Today* published a lengthy article on the strange sightings. Witnesses reported seeing a huge craftlike object behind the lights. Whatever it was, it moved slowly over Phoenix, stopped, and hovered. Since then, even the state's governor said he wanted an investigation. There have been subsequent and ongoing mass sightings of the same strange lights but no answers . . . yet.

UFO Watching:

There is no definite epicenter of UFO activity. But from newspaper reports and reports from UFO-investigation groups there do seem to be multiple sightings from the area of the **Gila River Indian Reservation,** which is just outside Phoenix in the Valley of the Sun. To get to the reservation, head east on I-10 toward Tucson. Take Exit 175 and follow signs to the Gila Arts & Craft Center. You can get visitor information by stopping here or by calling the center at 602-963-3981.

Another possible area to view the Phoenix lights is the stretch of highway on Interstate 10 between Phoenix and Casa Grande. From Phoenix, go south on Interstate 17 to I-10 heading east.

In downtown Phoenix, head to **Broadway Road/Southern Avenue around Fifty-first Avenue**—there were reports from that location as well.

For More Information:

Phoenix Visitors' Center, 602-254-6500.

SEDONA

If you're stressed out and want to lay your hands on some meditative rocks to rub or crystals to wear, there's only one place to go—Sedona. Located halfway between Phoenix and the Grand Canyon, this friendly but very touristy community hosts a large number of arts and cultural activities. But apparently artists and New-Agers aren't the only beings attracted to Sedona's extraordinary red rock landscape. Sedona is said to be—by numerous books, magazines, and its own citizens—a UFO sighting hot spot and (quick, imagine a wind chime tinkling as you read this) an area where spiritual contact with aliens takes place.

Native Americans believed Sedona was a holy and spiritual place. Today, believers say it's still a spiritual place and an attraction for UFOs because of the unusually high amount of electromagnetic energy held within the mountains. (Those in the know call it a vortex.) Even nonbelievers have to admit that the unusual red rock has a certain relaxing, meditative quality and that unusual lights and glowing objects can often be seen in the night skies.

An aerial view of Sedona— vortex and UFO hot spot.

UFO Watching:

Sighting areas change all the time here. But according to the local chamber of commerce, a good spot to view the sky is from **the road to the airport,** which is situated on the top of a high mesa in the middle of town. About halfway up this road is a small parking area. Airport Saddle Loop Trails is located up here. Hike a few minutes and you'll hit a great lookout area.

Tours:

For a guided extraterrestrial experience, contact **Starport Sedona** (520-282-7771)—the UFO organization in Sedona. They offer UFO tours, information, astrology readings, serious books, and wacky souvenirs. They have a ufologist in residence, Tom Dongo, and they publish a newsletter of current sighting areas available by subscription. If you have web access you can read all about the supposed out-of-this-world activity here at **www.starport-sedona.com.**

For More Information:

Sedona-Oak Creek Canyon Chamber of Commerce, 520-282-7722.

Arkansas
•••••••••••••

EUREKA SPRINGS

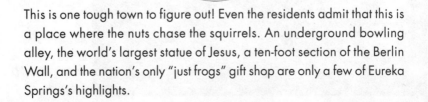

This is one tough town to figure out! Even the residents admit that this is a place where the nuts chase the squirrels. An underground bowling alley, the world's largest statue of Jesus, a ten-foot section of the Berlin Wall, and the nation's only "just frogs" gift shop are only a few of Eureka Springs's highlights.

But extraterrestrially speaking, this historic town, known for its healing waters, also plays host to one of the largest and best-known annual UFO conventions. **The Ozark UFO Conference** is where you will meet the experts, contactees, abductees, authors, and everyone else in between. It's usually held in April—call 501-354-2558 for information.

During the Day:

Even if you're not religious, you might want to visit the **Christ of the Ozarks** statue, because the seven-story statue is a sight to see. It's open year-round without charge. Over one million journey to view the statue annually. It is located off Highway 62 on Passion Play Road. Call 501-253-9200 for information.

For More Information:

Eureka Springs Tourist Center, 501-253-0505.

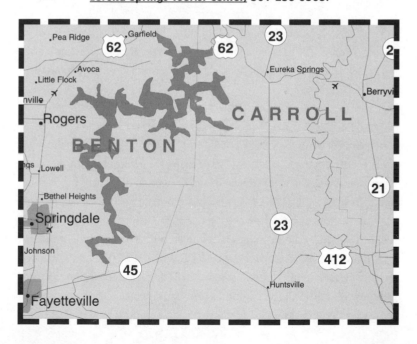

The infamous "Christ of the Ozarks" statue.

LITTLE ROCK

According to Lynne Bishop, MUFON state director for Arkansas, two of the most active UFO areas in this state are **Little Rock,** the state's capital, and heading to the north-central part, the small town of **Marshall.**

The Story:

Marshall is located in a predominately rural area located in the Boston Mountain Range of the Ozark Mountains. Bishop says that Marshall was quite a hot spot for many years, especially for triangular-shaped craft. However, it was discovered that this town was in a military flight zone. She believes now that the UFO reports are probably IFOs—military craft.

It's the state capital, however, that has the distinction of being home to more inexplicable sightings in the state and of being one of the few U.S. cities involved in the worldwide UFO wave of 1909–1910. According to an account described in several UFO encyclopedias, the sightings began in March 1909 on England's east coast and quickly spread across the globe. Witnesses consistently reported seeing a torpedo- or cigar-shaped object with some sort of a searchlight. It apparently hit the skies of Mabelvale, a small community just minutes away from Little Rock on December 13, 1910. A local resident reported seeing a bright, bobbing light that was moving rapidly through the sky. At first, German spies were the suspected culprits but that belief gave way to the speculation that what people across the globe may have been seeing was a UFO airship.

UFO Watching:
One of Little Rock's most popular skywatching spots is in **Pinnacle Mountain State Park,** located just outside of Little Rock on State Highway 10. The exact address is 11901 Pinnacle Valley Road, Roland, Arkansas 72135. Call 501-868-5806 for more information.

During the Day:
IMAX Theater, Aerospace Education Center, 3301 East Roosevelt Road, LR 72206; 501-376-IMAX or 501-371-0331.
University of Arkansas at Little Rock Planetarium, 2801 South University Avenue; 501-569-3259 or 569-3277.

For More Information:
Little Rock Visitors Bureau, 501-376-4781, 1-800-844-4781.

California
....
LOS ANGELES/TOPANGA CANYON

Topanga Canyon is thirteen miles northwest of Santa Monica and thirty miles west of Hollywood. It is located on State Highway 27, eight miles south of the 101 Ventura Freeway, five miles north of Pacific Coast

Highway. The canyon is famous for its scenery, and its alleged UFO activity. There has been on-again and off-again UFO activity here for many years, as reported in the local newspapers.

UFO Watching:

Head down Highway 27 toward Los Angeles for a good view of the sky. Due to the treacherous curves of Topanga Canyon Road, it's less dangerous to do your skywatching in the mountains. Good viewing spots can be found in the trails of the nearby **Santa Monica Mountains**—they rise above Los Angeles, widen to meet the curve of Santa Monica Bay, and reach their highest peaks facing the ocean.

According to the Santa Monica Mountains National Recreation Area National Park Service (805-370-2301), you can find great scenic vistas in nearby **Will Rogers State Park.** Numerous trails lead up into the mountain. Head about fifteen minutes out of Topanga on Topanga Canyon Road toward San Diego Freeway. Go south on the freeway and turn right on Sunset Boulevard. Go five or six miles, and you will come to the Will Rogers State Park.

During the Day:
The Los Angeles chapter of MUFON is exceptional for its general community outreach. Their monthly meetings are open to the general public and are really interesting (877-MUFONLA, or 626-450-MUFON). Meetings feature the latest information on UFO happenings, including sightings, research, and information on conferences and events. They also sponsor classes on how to be a UFO field investigator!

LOS FELIZ/THE GRIFFITH PARK OBSERVATORY

There are many Unidentified Walking Objects (UWOs) just roaming the streets of Los Angeles. But if you're looking for UFOs in the Los Angeles metropolitan area, your best bet is to head straight for the **Griffith Park Observatory** in Los Feliz for a fabulous view of the sky—day or night.

Resting comfortably on the southern slope of Mount Hollywood (where it offers a stunning view of the Los Angeles basin below), the observatory is a non profit, educational institution whose mission is to "provide information on astronomy and related sciences to the public" (according to the observatory's website, www.griffithobs.org/index.html). Since its construction in 1935, the observatory has been a major Los Angeles landmark, and is visited by nearly two million people each year. It offers three main attractions: the Hall of Science, the Telescopes, and the Planetarium Theater. All are open to the public and are free, except for the Planetarium shows.

The Site:
The Griffith Park Observatory (2800 East Observatory Road, Los Angeles, CA 90027–1255; 323-664-1191) is open Tuesday to Friday from 2 P.M. to 10 P.M. , Saturday and Sunday from 12:30 P.M. to 10 P.M., and closed Mondays from September through June, and open from 12:30 P.M. to 10 P.M. from July through August. Telescopes operate only when the sky is clear.

MOJAVE DESERT

You've heard of the power lunch and the power tie. But what about the power vortex? Well, you may experience one of these when you visit the following sites, located in the Mojave Desert about fifteen miles north of Yucca Valley—the **Giant Rock** and **Integratron.**

Giant Rock is, strangely enough, a giant rock. It's thought to be the biggest freestanding boulder in the world, and the Indians believed it was located on holy ground. They thought it symbolized the Great Spirit, as it was the largest single object in the area. Covering fifty-eight hundred square feet and standing seven stories high, it still is. But the Integratron gives it a run for its money—it's a 38-foot-high structure, 50 feet in diameter, that some believe is a rejuvenation machine.

The Story:

According to the Integratron's own literature and old articles written by George Van Tassel posted on the Integratron's official web site, here's the scoop: In the early 1940s, a mining prospector, Frank Critzer, obtained a claim from the U.S. government (they owned the land) around Giant Rock. Not having any money to build a shelter, Critzer dug out a huge hole, which eventually became a series of quite comfortable rooms under the boulder and moved in (or under). A German immigrant, some say Critzer was a spy during the war. Others say he was a brilliant but misunderstood thinker. He was killed in what many say was a mysterious dynamite accident.

In 1947 a friend of Critzer's, George Van Tassel, acquired the land. He was a former aircraft engineer who once worked as a test pilot for Howard Hughes and Douglas Aircraft.

Believing it was still a spiritual and holy place, Van Tassel began holding meditation sessions in 1953 at Giant Rock. He allegedly claimed that the sessions led to contacts with extraterrestrial beings. Van Tassel believed that he was taught an alien technique for rejuvenating living cell tissues. He and his family began building a structure they called the Integratron ostensibly to perform the rejuvenation.

The Integratron is a thirty-eight-foot-high, fifty-foot in diameter, non-metallic structure that Van Tassel believed was a rejuvenation machine. He spent eighteen years building the dome and claims to have relied heavily on research from the field of electromagnetics and from information received from regular ET changelings.

When Van Tassel died in 1978, a follower, Emil Canning, purchased the site. It's still used for meditation and UFO channeling and is open for tours and special workshops. Many "believers" have abandoned Giant Rock and the Integratron because they feel it's too "New-Agish" now. Other believers stick hard to the claim that there is a powerful vortex for physical and healing power under the dome. Whatever the truth may be, it's a very strange-looking and interesting place to visit even from an architectural point of view.

The Site:

The Integratron is located about two-and-a-half hours by car from Los Angeles. Take Interstate 10 east to California Highway, Exit 62, drive northeast about twenty-five minutes to the town of Yucca Valley. Turn left at Old Woman Springs Road which is Highway 247. Drive ten miles to Reche Road, where there is a large "Landers" sign on the right. Turn right and go about two miles to Belfield Road. Turn left and drive about one mile. The Integratron is at the end of Belfield Road at the intersection of Linn Road.

Open house is usually held once a month on a Sunday from 1 to 4 P.M. Suggested donation is $7 for adults, $2 for kids (under twelve years of age), and includes a one-hour tour of the facility, with a demonstration of some of the Dome technologies. You should always call to confirm that they will be open—707-522-9777. Camping on the grounds is only permitted during special workshops, and kitchen and bathing facilities are provided.

There are no motels, restaurants, or stores on the grounds but there are some located nearby in Yucca Valley and Joshua Tree. There is a National Park in Joshua Tree that is famous for its rockclimbing and is a great skywatching location. Campgrounds and back country camping are available.

For More Information:
Yucca Chamber of Commerce, 760-365-6323.
Joshua Tree Chamber of Commerce, 760-366-3723.

SAN DIEGO

The city of San Diego, and San Diego County in general, seem to have a fairly consistent number of UFO reports each year. San Diego is also the home of several UFO organizations.

According to local newspaper reports, in 1992, residents of San Diego woke up to discover their lights and appliances going on and off. It was said that a bright, glowing light was in the sky and pulsated in time to the lights and appliances. The gas and electric companies had no explanation.

A recent National UFO Reporting Center (NUFORC) case study, dated September 1998, discussed the alleged sighting of a fast-moving green-glowing object in Mira Mesa in San Diego County. The witness was near the Miramar Naval Air Station on Camio Ruiz Boulevard.

UFO Watching:

According to one local armchair astronomer, a popular San Diego sky-watching spot is outside the **Reuben H. Fleet Space Center and Planetarium** in Balboa Park. For more information contact the Balboa Park Visitors Center, 619-239-0512.

You might also want to contact the **San Diego UFO Society** for events, skywatching outings, and educational information. Call 619-299-9157. According to one of the society's two hundred members, there are several good skywatching spots along Sunrise Highway. Take Route 8 east out of the city and head north on the Sunrise Highway. There are pull-off sights for scenic viewing.

During the Day:

Interested in visiting with other cultures? Foreign dignitaries? Perhaps taking on an exchange student? Then visit the **Unarius Academy of Science** (145 South Magnolia Avenue, El Cajon, California, 1-800-475-7062) to learn about the Pleiadeans, an alien race who many believe will visit the Earth in 2001. UFO contactees and visionaries Ruth and Ernest Norman founded Unarius, a tax-exempt, nonprofit organization, in the 1950s. They started the academy to provide information about the nature of man and his progressive evolution (which will include man becoming a part of an interstellar community).

The academy houses a stunning collection of wall paintings and dioramas. Though their philosophy and teaching deals with self-healing, they have lately been preoccupied with preparing humankind for the

Pleiadean visit. With the help of the Pleiadeans, Earth is to be the thirty-third member of the Interplanetary Confederation, a vortex of great power made up of thirty-three worlds and the billions of people who are attuned to a higher frequency. Bring your headphones!

SAN FRANCISCO

The Golden Gate Bridge is considered by many to be the most famous bridge in the United States. But are more than tourists flocking to this beautiful Northern California city? That has lately been the question many residents have been asking.

The Story:
According to Radio Station KCBS, frantic callers were reporting an unidentified blue/white light streaking over the bay on August 4, 1998. The unknown object apparently broke into at least two pieces and disappeared going east. The local air control and meteorological monitoring center have (so far) no explanation for the sighting. Similar lights have been reported over the past couple of years.

UFO Watching:
For a great view of the bay (and maybe the strange object if you're lucky) head to San Francisco's famous **Pier 39.** Located on the northernmost point of the San Francisco peninsula, this is a great spot for views of the sky, Alcatraz, the Golden Gate and Bay Bridges. Telescopes are placed along the complex's perimeter road. To get there take the Bay Bridge to San Francisco. Stay to the left after Treasure Island. Take the first exit which is the Main Street/Embarcadero exit. At the bottom of the off-ramp, turn right at Harrison, go three blocks to the Embarcadero. Turn left and follow the street one-and-one-half miles.

Pier 39 will be on the right side of the street. Call (415) 981-PIER for more information.

Or head for the sky-high action at the nearby **Embarcadero Center's SkyDeck.** (The Center is a kind of mall with tons of restaurants and shops.) There is one heck of a view available here—hopefully, there won't be any earthquakes while you're on one of the indoor or outdoor observation decks.

Tickets may be purchased at the SkyDeck Ticket Booth located at One Embarcadero Center, Street Level. Tickets and more information are also available by calling for more information, please call SkyDeck at 888-737-5933 (888-SF-SKYDECK) or 415-772-0555.

Colorado

SALIDA

Was something unusual, possibly even extraterrestrial in the sky in Salida, Colorado, on August 27, 1995? Tim Edwards, a local resident, thinks there was. And he believes that he has the videotape that can prove it. According to Edwards's account, available through the Colorado MUFON organization's web site, he allegedly captured on videotape a bright shimmering white light that danced and darted over the skies of this quiet community. Another independent witness described it in a *Fate Magazine* interview as "a long, pencil-like, aluminum-foil triangle in the sky."

Edwards's tape has been analyzed and scrutinized by a team of experts that included an MIT physicist. They admitted it was compelling footage that can't be readily explained. Interestingly, a newspaper reported that in 1917 a local and respected citizen had seen a strange spinning object in the sky. An earlier visit perhaps?

The Site:

Edwards's restaurant, **ET's Landing** (1015 East Hwy. 50, Salida CO 81201, 719-539-1519), is done in alien decor and features an exhibit on UFOs. This is ground zero for Salida's purported UFO info and subsequent sighting information. It's located on Highway 50 near the big windmill.

For More Information:

Chaffee County Visitor's Guide, 800-831-8594.

SAN LUIS VALLEY

Pod people. The first publicized cattle mutilation case. Abductions. Phantom fires. Rumors of secret military bases. Hundreds of UFO sightings. According to local resident, investigator, and author Christopher O'Brien, for paranormal and possible out-of-this-world phenomena, it doesn't get any wackier than the San Luis Valley.

Even Big Foot is said to tread this 150-mile-by-45-mile-wide wishbone-shaped area in this area of south central Colorado and north central New Mexico. It's thus been dubbed the "mysterious valley."

Christopher O'Brien's popular book *The Mysterious Valley*, and his most recent book *Enter the Valley*, tell all about the alleged activity in fascinating detail. But here's a quick recap of the famous mutilated horse (much to the relief of cows, aliens it seems, are equal opportunity mutilators) that apparently got everyone talking about the purported happenings.

The Story:

According to O'Brien's accounts, on September 8, 1967, a local resident awoke to some devastating and frightening news. One of her favorite mares was supposedly found with her flesh missing from her shoulders to her nose. Her bones were allegedly bleached white as if they had been exposed to sunlight for a long, long period of time.

A satisfactory cause or motive has never been determined, but the owner did report frequent UFO sightings during that time. Since then, O'Brien has relentlessly documented and reported on what he says are the many waves of UFO sightings, mutilations, and strange flashing lights in the area.

Christopher O'Brien's Mysterious Valley web site at www.shell. rmi.net/~tmv gives the ongoing saga of strange doings in Colorado's San Luis Valley.

Cows from the San Luis Valley wait for something "udder-worldly."

UFO Watching:

O'Brien says that the **Great Sand Dunes National Monument** (11500 Highway 150, Mosca, CO) is the epicenter of UFO activity here. The sand dunes are more than seven-hundred-feet high so the view is terrific. It's located thirty-five miles northeast of Alamosa, Colorado, reached by U.S. Highway 160 and Colorado Highway 150 from the south; or from Colorado Highway 17 and County Six Mile Lane from the west.

> *"THE MATTER IS THE MOST HIGHLY CLASSIFIED SUBJECT IN THE UNITED STATES GOVERNMENT, RATING HIGHER EVEN THAN THE H-BOMB. FLYING SAUCERS EXIST. THEIR MODUS OPERANDI IS UNKNOWN BUT CONCENTRATED EFFORT IS BEING MADE BY A SMALL GROUP HEADED BY DR. VANNEVAR BUSH."*
>
> **Wilbert Smith, in a formerly classified Canadian government memorandum dated November 21, 1950**

The monument is open twenty-four hours a day, 365 days a year. Visitor center open daily, closed on winter holidays. There are camping facilities available. Call 719-378-2312 for more information.

For More Information:

The Alamosa County Chamber of Commerce and Visitor Center,
1-800-BLU-SKYS ext. 932, or 719-589-4840.

Connecticut

· · · · · · · · · · · ·

NORTH HAVEN

Connecticut isn't just for blue bloods anymore. It's also for green bloods, purple bloods, orange bloods, and any other color bloods, if you are to believe the UFO reports that have come from all over the state. Interested in Connecticut UFO country? Consider arranging your trip around the annual UFO Experience Conference in North Haven, Connecticut (located just over an hour from the city of Hartford and right next door to the better known New Haven).

The organizers of the conference, usually held in October, promise not only a stellar lineup of who's who in the UFO world, but also "a sup-

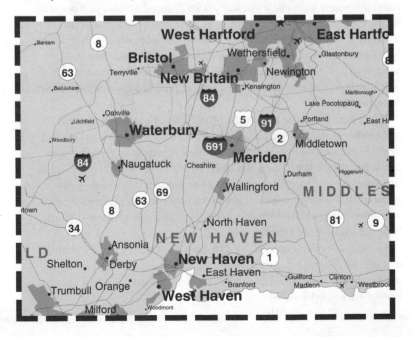

portive setting for people to 'unburden' themselves if they feel they have had UFO experiences but are afraid to talk about them." This conference is known for being good for non-technoids (read: regular folk).

Tickets for the two-day conference cost $125.00 and up. For more information and exact conference location, write Omega Communications, Box 2051, Cheshire, CT 06410 or fax 203-250-0501.

For More Information:
Greater New Haven Convention and Visitors Bureau, 800-332-STAY.

WHO ARE THE MEN IN BLACK?

Bridgeport, Connecticut's largest city, is said to be the birthplace of the **Men in Black** (MIB) legend. Back in 1953, resident Albert Bender ran an organization that investigated UFOs and published a small magazine on the subject. According to an article from *Astronet Review* (February 1992) Bender had announced that at least part of the mystery of flying saucers had been solved but could not be revealed. Soon after he gave an interview to a local paper stating that he was visited by "Three Men in Black" who warned him to stop his investigative activity. Bender later wrote a book about his visitors called *Flying Saucers and Three Men in Black*.

Much has been written about the MIBs. Though accounts differ somewhat, here's a generalized amalgam based on the wide body of literature: the MIB always travel in twos or threes, drive old black Cadillacs, dress in black suits, and have "inside information." Their mission is to silence and intimidate witnesses. They aren't overtly violent, just vaguely menacing and they sometimes leave the witness with physical symptoms such as blurred vision and headaches.

Some guess they are FBI or CIA agents. Others guess that they are aliens disguising themselves as government agents. MIBs walk with a strange limp, speak in strange voices, and convey a not-of-this-world aura.

WINSTED/TORRINGTON

According to an article in the *Hartford Courant,* the area about sixty miles north of North Haven is rumored to be a flap area for UFO activity.

Winsted and **Torrington** are two small communities that have had a number of alleged craft and nocturnal light sightings. According to MUFON reports, bright ovals have been seen landing on mountains near the area. Other glowing objects flashing with red and green lights have also been reported. Sightings have been reported along Route 8 between the two communities. The *Hartford Courant* reported that in a 1986 incident more than two hundred people watched as an airborne strip of lights illuminated the night sky over Highland Lake in Winsted. What, they wonder, did they see?

UFO Watching:

For good skywatching in Winsted, one local recommends an open field off Route 8 for a clear view of the skies. Take Route 8 to Route 44 west, make a left at the Dairy Queen, and you will see an open field on your left.

Delaware

....

DOVER

This infamous case comes right out of the USAF's Project Bluebook's files, which were made available to the public under the Freedom of Information Act. In 1964, just off the coast of Dover, Delaware, two air force pilots were flying on a USAF C-124 transport plane. They believe they saw a round, red-and-white object in the sky, and quickly realized that the strange object was on a collision course with them. The airplane evaded the object and the sighting lasted over two minutes. The air force was never able to determine what the object had been.

UFO Watching:

For some exciting skywatching head to **Dover Air Force Base.** However, this city's tourist bureau warns that if you see a UFO in Dover, it's most likely an IFO—the C-5 Galaxy, the largest cargo airplane in the free world. It's a regular and very cool feature in Dover's skies.

While you're there, visit the **The Air Mobility Command Museum,** 1301 Heritage Road, Dover AFB DE 19902-8001, open Monday through Saturday from 9 A.M. to 4 P.M. Free admission. Call 302-677-5938 for more information.

Florida

FLORIDA'S SPACE COAST

If anyone's going to meet an extraterrestrial in their own homes, it'll be the folks here on the seventy-two-mile stretch of coastal land known as Florida's famous "Space Coast." Walt Disney World is only forty-five minutes to the west and Miami is three hours from the west. To get to the Space Coast directly from Interstate 95, take exits 70 through 81 or from Orlando, go east on the Bee Line Expressway (528) to A1A.

The Space Coast's most famous attraction is the **NASA Kennedy Space Center.** At the NASA Kennedy Space Center, earthlings may tour the launch area by bus, see IMAX movies, walk among authentic vintage spacecraft, or even observe a real-life launch! The seventy-acre, out-of-this-world attraction is located on Florida's Space Coast one hour east of Orlando. There are no admission or parking fees to enter the Visitor Complex. To receive a brochure, call 407-452-2121, extension 4132. For launch information, call 1-800-KSC-INFO in Florida only.

The Kennedy Space Center Visitor Complex is located off State Road 405, NASA Parkway, six miles inside the Space Center entrance. Take State Road 528, the Bee Line, east if coming from Orlando. Use Exit 78 northbound or 79 southbound off Interstate 95. Use State Road 3 on Merritt Island if approaching from the south. Always follow signs for "Kennedy Space Center."

Also on the Space Coast is the **Astronaut Memorial Planetarium and Observatory** (1519 Clearlake Road, Cocoa, Florida 32922; 407-634-3732). They have public viewings and educational programs. It's located on the Cocoa Campus of Brevard Community College.

The Astronaut Hall of Fame (6225 Vectorspace Boulevard, Titusville, Florida 32780; 407-269-6100) is home to the largest collection of astronauts' personal artifacts (but hopefully not toothbrushes and dirty socks) in the world!

Located just west of NASA's Kennedy Space Center, the U.S. Astronaut Hall of Fame is the only facility in the nation dedicated exclusively to telling the stories of America's astronauts. From Orlando: Travel east on the Bee Line Expressway (S.R. 528) to Challenger Memorial Parkway (S.R. 407). Follow Challenger Memorial Parkway to Columbia Drive (S.R. 405). Follow Columbia Drive past U.S. 1, and the U.S. Astronaut Hall of Fame is on your right.

The Hall of Fame is also home to **U.S. Space Camp Florida,** where young people from across the world experience some of the thrill of astronaut training in a fun, hands-on learning environment. Their number is 800-63-SPACE.

The U.S. Space Walk of Fame, also in Titusville, overlooks the Kennedy Space Center. This riverwalk preserves America's history in space through a progressive maze of memorabilia, interpretive plaques, and art. The waterfront terrace of the riverwalk has become a popular viewing platform during NASA shuttle liftoffs. Call 407-267-1141 for more information, and ask for Ray Smith—Walk of Fame VP.

For More Information:
The Official Accommodations Guide of the Orlando Area,
Orlando/Orange County Convention and Visitors Bureau, Inc.,
1-800-551-0181 or 407-363-5872.

GULF BREEZE

Though it's never been proven that what people see in these skies are alien craft, there are, according to dozens of newspapers, UFO investigative groups, and eyewitness accounts, UFOs in the skies here. Gulf Breeze is most definitely one of the nation's hottest hot spots for sightings of the unidentified kind.

The Story:

Located on a beautiful peninsula and situated between Pensacola and Santa Rosa Island, this once sleepy town became the focus of an out-and-out UFO controversy in November 1987, with the publication of a series of Polaroid shots taken by a local contractor. Hundreds of sightings have been reported since then, with dozens more photos and videotapes to support them. Many feel that the contractor's photos provide incontrovertible proof that UFOs are real.

> **Factoid: The most common type of UFO hoax is a prank balloon, which involves tying a flare or candle to a helium-filled balloon. Once in the air it will make the balloon look like a glowing orb streaking in the sky.**

Others say "no way." The first doubt arose after a Styrofoam UFO model was allegedly found in the attic of the contractor's former residence. The model strongly resembled a drawing he had made of one of his UFO sightings. A local teenager later came forward and claimed that he helped fake the photos. The contractor says this is part of a cover-up.

But whether or not you believe him, there are UFOs flying around in this part of Florida—exactly what their origin is or is not has still not been determined.

UFO Watching:

According to Topper Jones, a Gulf Breeze Research Team member, almost every night a group meets at **Shoreline Park** to skywatch. It's a great place to watch with other interested people, but anywhere you can see the sky in the Gulf Breeze/Pensacola Beach area is excellent. Jones says that there have been many sightings all over the area.

From Three-Mile Bridge take a right at the second light into the park. Head toward the recreation center and then toward the water on your left. There are always groups out and about, watching the skies for UFOs. Check out the team's web site for the latest UFO news from the Gulf Breeze at **http://gulfbreezeufos.com**.

During the Day:
The National Museum of Naval Aviation (1750 Radford Boulevard, Pensacola, FL; 800-327-5002) is one of the world's largest air and space museums. It's open every day from 9 A.M. to 5 P.M., free admission. Follow the history of naval aviation from wooden planes to the Skylab Module. The adjoining IMAX Theatre shows big-screen aviation films that make you feel like you're in the cockpit (not for those prone to motion sickness). From Gulf Breeze, take Route 98 over Bay Bridge from Gulf Breeze to Pensacola mainland, this is Bayfront Parkway, which turns into Main Street, turn left onto Barrancas, turn left onto Navy Boulevard, and you will see the signs.

For More Information:
Gulf Breeze Visitor's Information, 850-932-7888.

WEST PALM BEACH

With its sultry weather, sandy beaches, and gently waving palm trees, Florida has always been a vacationer's paradise. And UFO fans won't be disappointed here either. Get ready to see more than pink flamingos.

The Story:
The International Society for UFO Research reported that a local resident allegedly saw a brightly colored moon-shaped object darting around in

the skies on January 12, 1998. He was just off the pier in the downtown area in the early evening.

West Palm Beach was also the site of either one of the best UFO hoaxes in history or one of the creepiest close encounters. They are still dissecting this case at the UFO conventions and in publications. Folks still argue about this one-over their early-bird specials, of course.

According to accounts in several books, including *The Encyclopedia of UFOs* edited by Ronald D. Story, the incident goes like this:

August 19, 1952: A scoutmaster was returning from a trip when he thought he saw a plane going down into some trees. He stopped to investigate, leaving his troop behind in the car. When he walked into a clearing, he says he felt a blast of sudden heat, as if he had just walked into an oven. When he looked above him, he said he saw a flat surface of a large round object. The scoutmaster felt as if his muscles and reflexes were suddenly impaired. Suddenly, a red fireball came out of the craft and floated toward him. He threw his arms over his face. It blinded him momentarily and smelled horrible. The scoutmaster passed out.

By the time he came to, the purported mysterious craft was gone and the sheriff had arrived on the scene. The only evidence of what had happened were burn marks left on the scoutmaster's cap and the fact that the hair on his forearms had been singed off. Was he telling the truth or not? The scouts waiting in the car reportedly did confirm his story. They said after they saw the fireball hit their scoutmaster that they had become frightened (what a bunch of babies!) and had called the sheriff.

Analysis on the cap showed that it probably wasn't being worn at the time the burns were made. The scoutmaster's dubious background and the fact that he seemed to relish the publicity would seem to indicate that the event was a hoax. However, an analysis of the grass around the area did reveal evidence of having been heated at a high temperature, supporting the validity of the report. Thus, this case remains a real head-scratcher that has never been resolved.

UFO Watching:

Head to **John D. MacArthur State Park** (State Road 703, Singer Island, North Palm Beach, FL 561-624-6950)—this park has 1.8 miles of secluded beach with excellent viewing opportunities.

Also, the Palm Beach Bike Trail runs along the intracoastal side of Palm Beach and provides some of Palm Beach's most awesome views.

During the Day:

It's worth a visit to the **South Florida Science Museum**—it houses the Aldrin Planetarium and Gibson Observatory (4801 Dreher Tail North, West Palm Beach, Florida 33405; 561-832-1988). Don't miss the Pink Floyd light show.

Georgia

LA GRANGE

This is one heck of a hot spot. Read all about it in tons of newspapers, including the *Atlanta Journal Constitution,* which always keeps abreast of this area's UFO happenings.

LaGrange, Georgia (pop. 27,000) sits on the shore of West Point Lake in west central Georgia. This town, about sixty miles southwest of Atlanta, is filled with historic landmarks, fine architecture, and lots of folks who claim to have seen UFOs. LaGrange is located along the Troup-Heard Corridor (THC) which has long been famous for its alleged UFO activity.

The International Society for UFO Research (ISUR) is the group that's been heavily investigating goings-on here. (To learn more, visit their most excellent web site at www.isur.com.) These folks hardly get a day off because this is actually a big area with a lot of sky activity. It stretches from east to west for approximately 120 miles and south to north for seventy miles; the THC encompasses an area larger than Massachusetts. According-

ing to local MUFON director, Jim Thompson, UFO reports have been documented in LaGrange and the THC since before World War II. In 1938, a teenager reported seeing a domed saucer with portholes in the

Factoid: About 300 soldiers from the Confederate Army of Tennessee are buried here—maybe the EBEs are history buffs. . . .

middle of the day. According to the soon-to-be WWII combat infantryman, the craft was as large as a commercial jetliner of today.

Recent photographs, videos, and tons of witnesses leave little doubt that years later LaGrange is still a hotbed of UFO activity. There are fireballs, giant saucers, tubelike objects, and other kinds of UFOs here. Alien craft or not, the skies sure are busy in this part of Georgia.

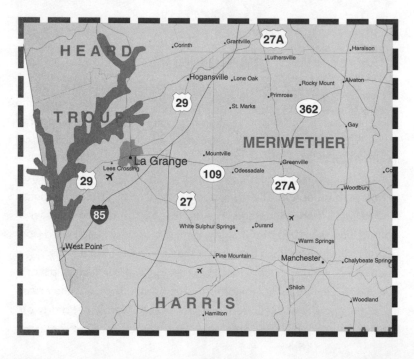

OF PRESIDENTS AND UFOs

If you want proof that all kinds of people from all walks of life think they have seen UFOs, just visit **Leary, Georgia** (about two hundred miles south of Atlanta). Go to the center of town (it isn't hard to find) and ask one of the locals about its claim to fame—he or she will probably tell you that Leary is where the famous **Jimmy Carter UFO sighting** took place.

According to files released by the FBI under the Freedom of Information Act (and available for public viewing on the FBI's own web site, www.fbi.gov), the sighting took place on the evening of January 6, 1969. The then-governor saw what he considered to be a UFO. "I am convinced that UFOs exist because I have seen one," Carter reported to the FBI. "It was big; it was bright; it changed colors; and it was about the size of the moon."

The purported sighting got a lot of media coverage at the time and was investigated by the National Investigations Committee on Aerial Phenomena. At the time, however, UFO debunkers claimed that Carter's account matched the position of the planet Venus. Carter apparently disagreed, because when he became president he requested that NASA evaluate whether a new UFO probe was warranted—so there!

UFO Watching:

So Many Spots, So Little Time. A THC expert and local resident, Jim Thompson, recommends the following skywatching areas: Pine Mountain in Harris County and lake sites near West Point Dam in West Troup County. North of there, near the Troup-Heard County line, Roosevelt State Park in Pine Mountain offers excellent viewing from its twelve-hundred-feet high hills. Cannonville and Stovall in Troup, near Hogg Mountain, off Bartley Road is also good if someone will let you get on his or her property. But by and large, Thompson says the most consistent sightings

AND IF ASTRONAUT OUTERWEAR IS YOUR THING . . .
Travel a short ways to the bigger town of Albany. Go twenty-two miles east on State Road 62 to State Road 91 and you're there. Visit the Thronateeksa Heritage Center (100 Roosevelt Avenue, Albany, GA 3170; 912-432-6955) which houses southwest Georgia's only planetarium, the Wetherbee. One of their claims to fame is a display of the space suit worn by astronaut Charlie Duke while training for his space mission. Duke, lunar module pilot for Apollo 16, is one of only twelve men to have walked on the moon.

have taken place along the Troup-Heard County line. This is the "guts" of the Troup-Heard Corridor and why it is named as such.

If you've had your Wheaties for breakfast and think you're up for it, you could take the "THC Circuit Challenge." If driving, leave La Grange, continue to obey local traffic laws, and go north on Highway 219 until reaching Franklin in Heard County. Franklin can be reached from Highway 219 by crossing the Chattahoochee River—go about five miles and turn right (east) on Bevis Road or continue on Highway 219 north until it dead-ends into Highway 34 and then turn right. To return to La Grange, take Highway 27 south. Excellent UFO sightings have been made near any of the water crossings between Franklin and La Grange on Highway 27. The New River and Potato Creek crossings have had the most sightings. Other good spots are on Highway 100 near Corinth and anywhere in western Troup and Heard Counties.

According to Thompson, the worst time to see a UFO in the THC is Friday or Saturday night. The best time is late Sunday night or early Monday morning. The bulk of UFOs have appeared after 10 P.M. on weeknights.

You can read about the latest reports of supposed UFO activity in this area on the International Society for UFO Research's web site at www.isur.com.

Hawaii

MAUI

You don't only need to look on the beach to find great bodies here—look up in the sky for a few unidentified bodies to gawk at. Here's one of Hawaii's most notorious UFO stories.

The Story:

A couple was relaxing on a Maui beach in January of 1975 when they noticed a strange object approaching in the sky. According to the couple's description, which was reported in the *International UFO Reporter* (May/June 1990), it was square with a domed top and bottom. It made no sound and had no wings or other visible means of propulsion. They thought they saw a row of lights along its upper edge. The man managed to snap three photographs of the unusual object before it sped over the mountains and out of sight. When he returned home, he had the film developed and sent it

> **"I BELIEVE THAT THESE EXTRATERRESTRIAL VEHICLES AND THEIR CREWS ARE VISITING THIS PLANET FROM OTHER PLANETS WHICH OBVIOUSLY ARE A LITTLE MORE . . . ADVANCED THAN WE ARE . . . "**
>
> *Colonel L. Gordon "Gordo" Cooper, Mercury 7 Astronaut (in a letter to the United Nations, 1978)*

to NASA. A NASA official responded that the image could have been sunlight reflecting off the large rotor of a helicopter. The couple was not satisfied with that answer.

Incredibly, fourteen and a half years later on July 7, 1989, a Tokyo couple videotaped a UFO similar to the one captured on film that day on Maui. The Tokyo sighting was investigated by local news reporters who contacted a local air base. There was no radar contact and the object on

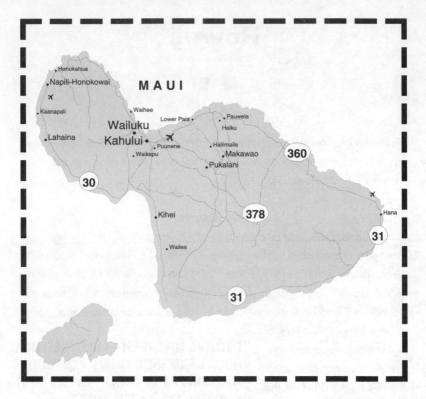

the video remains a mystery. The link between these cases, however, is considered significant because there are so few cases in which individuals have photographed almost identical UFOs at very different times and locations.

UFO Watching:

For premium skywatching head to the **West Maui Mountains.** The views are spectacular of both the land and the sea.

You can also watch for UFOs while participating in water sports and whale watching! Call **UFO Parasailing,** 808-661-7UFO.

For More Information:
Hawaii Visitor's Guide, 800-GO-HAWAII.

OAHU

This scenery here is right off of a postcard. The Koolau Mountains are the backdrop practically everywhere you look. But nestled inside Haiku Valley is the coast guard's Omega Station. This was once used to help navigate aircraft and ships literally around the world. But some people are wondering if its huge cables were attracting UFOs to the island? Hmmmmm . . .

The Story:

There was a flap that occurred here in 1995 that lasted for several days. The *Contact with Non-human Intelligence Agency* (CNI News—an electronic newsletter) ran a February 6, 1995 article detailing the events. Many residents reported seeing strange lights and flying discs around the station. The coast guard has since closed the station (in 1997), but UFO reports have persisted. The *Hawaii Star Bulletin* reported on March 27, 1998 that residents of Oahu were treated to a spectacular light show with bright colors in the skies. Police dispatchers had many reports of what officials said could have been space junk, a meteor, or a fireball (fireballs are known to light the skies around here periodically). Of course, the phenomenon could have been caused by something else— something not of this world. There is also a marine station located several miles directly east of the Omega, which has been the scene of supposed UFO activity.

UFO Watching:

The area where people have been seeing strange lights and flying discs is easily reached from Honolulu. Take the Likelike Highway into Oahu, you will pass near the station and then you pass via tunnel through the **Koolau Mountains.** You can skywatch at the base of the mountain when you come through the tunnel.

Idaho

· · · · · · · · · · · ·

MALAD

Are there UFOs in Malad? This is a question some residents have been asking themselves here for a long time. Frightened school children witnessed saucer-shaped craft in the sky. And then there's the rumor of secret tests taking place in a cave located in nearby **Weston Canyon.**

The buzz—according to several written accounts, and a local who wishes to remain anonymous—is that the military has hidden alien ships and bodies here. There's another local who has claimed to have seen

them. There have been military vehicles seen here, and residents have reported underground explosions in the cave. (Approach this area with extreme caution.)

The Site:
The Cave is eight miles east of Malad in Weston Canyon on the north side of the road. The cave is off the road. It's huge and hard to miss. Malad Valley, in Oneida County, is located in the southeastern part of Idaho, very close to the Utah state line.

RIRIE

If you're looking for a really juicy case, complete with encounters, confrontations, levitation, animal reaction, carjacking, and more, head for Ririe, Idaho. Located in the southeast corner of Jefferson County, just thirty miles northeast of Idaho Falls. Nearby attractions include several of Idaho's most famous outdoor recreational opportunities. With a population of 632, Ririe is really a friendly and slow-paced community. This is the kind of place where type-A personalities become type B—unless you meet an unwanted visitor along Highway 26.

The Story:
You can read more about this chilling tale, a case described in the fascinating book *Uninvited Guests* by Richard Hall. Two young men were riding on Highway 26 when suddenly, their account alleges, a bright light blinded them. Out of the light emerged a small domed craft. The dome was transparent and two small aliens were in plain view. The car lost power and stopped.

One of the aliens emerged from the dome. It was purported to be a strange little being with small eyes, a slitlike mouth, and large ears who carjacked the duo. The alien proceeded to telepathically direct the car into a field while the frightened pair cowered in the passenger seat. One man bolted and ran to a nearby farmhouse. But the other was frozen in shock. He reported that the being emitted high-pitched, unintelligible sounds. A second alien chased the man who ran but must have changed his or her mind. When he or she returned to the car both beings floated back up to the craft. It disappeared as suddenly as it appeared. Talk about uninvited guests!

Supporting evidence of the encounter: Local farmers reported that their cattle seemed distressed and had bolted for unknown reasons. Another witness was found who reported a similar encounter that same night.

UFO Watching:
Highway 26 from Idaho Falls is very rural, dark, and wide open—so you'll have plenty of open sky to watch.

SNAKE RIVER CANYON

One of the earliest UFO sightings to catch the attention of the air force took place along the Snake River near Idaho's Twin Falls on August 13, 1947.

The Story:
According to accounts in several UFO encyclopedias, an area resident had sent two young boys to get some rope that he had left in his boat. When the boys failed to return, the man headed down to the river to look for them. He found them staring up into the sky at an object that resembled an inverted pie pan. An odorless, smokeless exhaust flame was coming out from the object, which was about twenty feet in diameter and the same color as the sky. However, because these witnesses were in the

┌───┐
WHO THE HECK IS EDDY?
Eddy (noun): A current moving contrary to the direction of the main current, especially in a circular motion.
└───┘

canyon, which is about four-hundred-feet deep and twelve-hundred-feet wide, they could see it against the rocks. As it passed over the trees it didn't bend them as the wind might, they later said, but spun the trees around as if they were in a vacuum.

The air force, believing that the witnesses were credible and truthful, conducted an investigation. They concluded that the three saw a rapidly moving atmospheric eddy.

UFO Watching:

You can skywatch, camp, and climb in the nearby **City of Rocks National Reserve** (208-824-5519), which features granite columns—some looming sixty stories high. (For some reason granite is supposedly to aliens like peanuts are to elephants.) Season runs April to November.

For another good skywatching spot head to nearby **Shoshone Falls.** Considered "The Niagara of the West," the falls plummets fifty-two feet farther than Niagara. October through April is the best time to view the falls.

During the Day:

The Herrett Center for Arts and Sciences houses the Faulkner Planetarium (The College of Southern Idaho, 315 Falls Avenue, Twin Falls, ID 83303-1238; 208-736-3059.) This is the largest planetarium in Idaho and one of the most up-to-date in the nation, with a fifty-foot dome, forty-nine slide projectors, and a six-thousand-watt sound system.

For More Information:

Twin Falls Area Chamber of Commerce, 800-255-8946.

Illinois

....

CHICAGO

Ever wonder where the terms *close encounter* and *close encounter of the third kind* come from? Head to the **J. Allen Hynek Center for UFO Studies** (2457 W. Peterson, Chicago, IL 60659; 773-271-3611) and you'll find out. You'll also discover the world's largest library of UFO reports, documents, books, and research. The Center for UFO Studies was started by Dr. J. Allen Hynek, who was a professor of astronomy at Ohio State University, and later became chairman of the astronomy department at Northwestern University. He became famous for his involvement as the astronomical consultant to the United States Air Force's Project Bluebook.

At first, Dr. Hynek was skeptical of the reality of extraterrestrial sightings, but became convinced that UFOs were worthy of serious study. In 1972, Dr. Hynek published his famous book, *The UFO Experience: A Scientific Study*, in which he coined the phrase *close encounters*. In 1973, he started the Center for UFO Studies and served as its scientific director until his death in 1986.

CUFOS maintains an extensive library and archive of UFO-related materials. These materials include books, articles, documents, and sighting reports. Scientists working with the organization also investigate sightings and other UFO-related reports.

COLLINSVILLE

There are few spots in the United States that invoke the mystery of Stonehenge, but **Cahokia Mounds State Historic Site,** which preserves the most sophisticated prehistoric native civilization north of Mexico, comes pretty close. Within the twenty-two-hundred-acre tract, located a few miles west of Collinsville, Illinois, lie the archaeological remnants of the central section of the ancient settlement that is today known as Cahokia.

This is not an official viewing spot for UFOs (although skywatching is excellent here) but it has attracted the attention of some in the UFO community. Some people say there is something just plain mysterious about this spot. The ancients who lived here most definitely had a relationship with the skies. Recent discoveries of posts that archeologists have dubbed "Woodhenge" are thought to have had alignments with certain bright stars or the Moon.

The Site:

The Cahokia Mounds are located about eight miles from downtown St. Louis near Collinsville, Illinois. You can reach it via Interstates 55-70 and

255, and Illinois 111, on Collinsville Road. It is open daily free of charge. Call 618-346-5160 for more information or a Calendar of Events.

Indiana

·············

BLOOMINGTON

If you know anything about alien abductions, you know Bud Hopkins. And if you don't, you will in a few paragraphs. Bud is *the* name in abduction investigations. He's a professional investigator who has looked into hundreds of alleged abductions over the years—and he's convinced that it's happening.

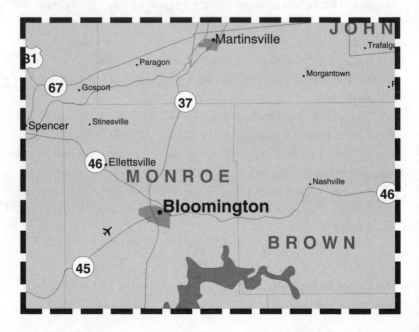

The Story:

Hopkins was so impressed by an Indiana woman's description of her repeated abductions that he wrote a book about her—*Intruders*. It was later made into a TV movie and was the first in-depth book on the subject. At the time, the subject of the book was Kathie Davis, but her name had been changed to protect her identity. Now we know that her name is really Debbie Jordan, and that she lives just outside of Indianapolis. Don't look her up in person, but she does have an extensive web site **(www.debshome.com)** and has now dedicated herself to writing, speaking, researching, and spreading the word about alleged alien activity and abduction.

In December 1977, Debbie was allegedly taken from her car by a group of aliens. The other occupants had been "switched off" or "knocked out" so that they would have no awareness of the abduction. She was taken upon a flying saucer and given the first of many gynecological examinations. Hopkins believes it's possible that the aliens inseminated Debbie, and that the fetus was later removed during another abduction. Analysis of the abductions relies, as it does for most abduction cases, on regression hypnosis.

UFO Watching:

You can't go to Debbie's house, but you can visit the **Bloomington area,** which is forty-five miles from Indianapolis. This area is said to be the home to a brilliant, multicolored light that hovers, floats, and rapidly disappears. Other craftlike objects have also been reported in Bloomington and its surrounding areas. Bloomington is on Indiana Highway 46 about fifty miles (eighty kilometers) southwest of Indianapolis.

Head for **Griffy Lake Nature Preserve,** Headly and Hinkle Road. A nature preserve comprised of a 109-acre lake and twelve hundred acres of woodlands. Twin Lakes Sports Park located on West Second Street, just east of the 37 bypass, features an elevated observation space so bring the binos.

MONGO

Reports of UFO sightings ebb and flow, even in nontraditional UFO areas like Mongo, Indiana (and not surprisingly, they have increased since *The X-Files* was launched). Mongo is located in the heart of the Pigeon River Fish and Game Wildlife Preserve—the perfect out-of-the-way spot for close encounters.

The Story:

In one 1994 Mongo report investigated by the Indiana MUFON group, six men were just hanging out at the Trading Post Canoe Rental, a local canoe livery and campground located in the heart of the Pigeon River Fish and Game Wildlife Preserve (it's about the only place to go in and around Mongo).

Suddenly, a light appeared in the western sky and then—boom—a UFO was hovering 150 feet above their heads. According to one of the campers, the craft appeared to be a cylinder with a large dome on top. It slowly maneuvered back and forth. The men claimed that the craft projected a bright translucent light. Before it sped off, the craft lowered and paused. The men noticed that the object became more translucent, as if gathering power. A red light flashed three times and—boom—the UFO vanished.

Several other people reported seeing the same object that night. The local newspaper later reported that the "UFO" was really a blimp, which happened to be passing over the area. The witnesses, who all claim to have seen blimps before, think that explanation is, well, full of hot air. They are now confirmed believers.

HOW TO DEFEND YOURSELF AGAINST AN ABDUCTION
1. Just say "no"! You have to be confident to pull it off, but it often works. Your lexicon of phrases should include commands such as, "Go away!," "Leave me alone!," or "Beat it ET—go home!"
2. Use physical resistance. Your intent should never be to kill or seriously injure an alien, but rather to let them know that their presence is violating your right to privacy. Go for their big red eyes.
3. Always carry St. John's Wort with you—to aliens, it's like garlic is to vampires, and it will keep you from getting depressed as well.
4. Use metaphysical resistance. Picture yourself enveloped in a protective shield of white light. Telepathic aliens may get the message.

Adapted from *How to Defend Yourself Against Alien Abduction* by UFO researcher Ann Druffel (Three Rivers Press).

The Sites:

Mongo is about forty-two miles north of Forth Wayne just off State Road 3. **The Trading Post** (219-367-2493) is located one block west of Mongo on the river.

During the Day:

Give Me Space (101 S. Detroit Street, LaGrange, IN 46761; 219-463-UFOS), a great little gift store located on the south east corner of the nearby town of LaGrange (6 miles west of Mongo, across from the LaGrange County Courthouse). They offer a strange, but handy, mix of science fiction, fantasy and gaming supplies.

For More Information:

<u>La Grange County Convention and Visitors Bureau,</u>
1-800-254-8090.

Iowa

DES MOINES

The capital city of Iowa is the third-largest insurance center in the world with nearly sixty insurance companies calling it home. And if that's not enough to entice you to visit, maybe the fact that Des Moines is also home to several well-documented UFO sightings will draw you in.

The Story:

One recent sighting (as reported to Iowa's chapter of MUFON) occurred on November 11, 1997. Two Iowa State college students driving back to Ames, Iowa (a city on Highway 69 about twenty-eight miles north of Des Moines) spotted a strange object in the sky—a dark orange globe of light. At first, they thought the light was resting on a water tower nearby, but this proved to be an illusion. They continued driving and then caught sight of a full circular orb ahead of them—moving fast. The object finally seemed to shoot into the horizon and disappear over its edge.

UFO Watching:

Skywatching is a breeze in Des Moines—just visit the **Ashton Observatory.** It's located twenty minutes northeast of Des Moines on Highway F17 just off of Highway 330, west of Baxter. The site has superior viewing avenues in all directions. The observatory houses two permanently mounted telescopes. The twin-domed facility has a sixteen-inch, f/4.5 Newtonian, and a ten-inch, f/10, computer-aided, Schmidt-Cassegrain (read: some really powerful scopes). There are also five outdoor telescope pads.

During the Day:

For a tour of Iowa's most beautiful cow and pig farms contact: **Madison County Farm and Country Tours,** 1510 270th Street, Winterset, IA 50273; 515-462-3515.

For More Information:

The Convention and Visitors Bureau's Hotel Hotline, 515-287-4396.

GARRISON/CEDAR RAPIDS

?

In 1947, a railroad engineer saw ten shiny disc-shaped objects fluttering along Cedar Rapids's skies in a string. Several years later, a very interesting and important event would take place in the same area—the infamous **Barr incident.** This unusual case occurred, according to UFO researcher/editor Ronald Story, on a bean field in Garrison, just outside of Cedar Rapids.

The Story:

Two young girls were inside the Barr family farmhouse on July 13, 1969, when they reportedly saw bright lights flashing in the windows. When they looked outside, they were stunned to see a saucer-shaped craft descending into a nearby field. By the time they and several other witnesses reached the field, the UFO was already back in the sky. It hovered for a moment and raced away. But it did leave what many believe to be a landing trace—a ring of burned grass. Investigators from the then-well-known Aerial Phenomena Research Organization (APRO) investigated the scene. Some analysts of the burned grass believed that it could have been faked, but others said it showed evidence of being burned with something that generated much more heat than any earth source could have produced.

This case provides what some say is that rare and elusive physical evidence skeptics are always calling for.

UFO Watching:

Head for the fields just outside of town. The farmhouse is gone, but it's still dark and creepy and if you take a nice picnic dinner, you won't mind.

During the Day:

If you visit Cedar Rapids, Iowa's second-largest city, you may want to consider going in September—when the **Marion's Swamp Fox Festival** is held. Festival events change each year, but usually include parades, exhibits, demonstrations, history walks, athletic events, food, and corny entertainment.

Kansas

....

ABILENE

Abilene's reputation as the "wickedest and wildest town in the West" was forged as hundreds of cowboys arrived in town along the historic Chisholm Trail during the late 1800s. They sure could whoop it up in the town's numerous saloons. Now, the town's a lot quieter, a lot more sober and known for its charming historic district—although every now and then, this town gets it share of UFOs whooping it up in the skies above.

The Story:

This case was well documented, and a good summary appears in Richard Hall's popular book *Uninvited Guests*. In 1965, a truck driver was heading north on Highway 15 about twenty-five miles south of Abilene. His headlights blinked and failed just as, out of nowhere, a large object allegedly swooshed overhead and landed on the roadway ahead of him. The trucker slammed on his breaks to avoid a collision. To his surprise, an orange UFO was allegedly hovering just above the road surface. It was disc-shaped, with a domed top and square windows.

A car coming in the opposite direction stopped as well. The driver got out of his car and headed for the truck. But before these witnesses could compare notes, the UFO reportedly emitted sparks and made a whistling sound. It took off toward the west, then turned south. Both drivers hit the road and didn't look back. Later the truck driver reported the sighting to the Abilene police, who had received similar reports of sparking and swooshing activity in the skies over the city.

UFO Watching:

Abilene is located at the end of the junction of Interstate 70 and K-15 Highways. There have been a few UFO reports from drivers in this area, although **Highway 15** south of Abilene is probably a hotter area.

DELPHOS

Welcome to Delphos, Kansas. This small farming community is located in northern Ottawa County within the beautiful Solomon River Valley, and is the site of a mysterious close encounter.

The Story:

This has been a widely publicized case. According to an account given by the highly regarded researcher and writer Jerome Clark, on November 2, 1971, at around 7 P.M., a sixteen-year-old boy was tending to some sheep on the family farm. He heard a strange rumbling noise. Then he saw a brightly illuminated object, about seventy-five feet away, hovering two feet over the ground. The boy reported that the object was about ten feet in diameter. It glowed with multicolored lights and had a bulge in the middle.

The light emanating from it was so bright that it hurt the boy's eyes and he was temporarily blinded. When he regained his sight, he saw that the UFO was now in the sky. He ran to get his parents. When they went to the spot their son pointed out, they found a glowing ring on the ground. They also said the trees nearby were glowing as well. After touching the soil that they described as cool and moist, the couples' fingers allegedly went numb (and they stayed that way for several days).

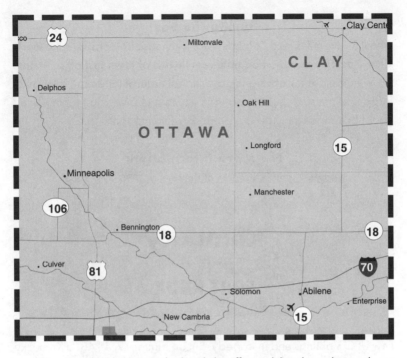

The day after the event, the local sheriff noted that the soil was almost pure white. Several days later, Ted Phillips, a well-known UFO investigator, sampled the soil. Amazingly, the soil remained dry—despite the fact that snow had fallen upon it. Upon further analysis, it was found that the soil was, for unknown and inexplicable reasons, resistant to moisture.

Even today, there remains no satisfactory answer for what really happened at Delphos. The boy claims to have seen additional craft and to have had subsequent and frequent contacts with aliens in the area.

UFO Watching:

State Highway K-41 is the primary route into Delphos, and is a great skywatching route. If you stop in town, ask for directions to the old Johnson farm—but make sure you ask the owners for permission before poking around.

During the Day:

About twelve miles from Delphos, near Minneapolis, Kansas, is the **Rock City Park** (two-and-a-half miles southwest of town just off Interstate 135—there are tons of signs), a national natural landmark filled with large and unusual rock formations which will give you that mystical, goose-bumpy feeling. This is a great skywatching spot.

For More Information:

Ottowa County Chamber of Commerce, 785-392-3068.

Kentucky

FORT KNOX

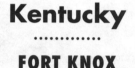

Few UFO sightings end in tragedy. But on January 7, 1948, a Kentucky National Guard pilot, Captain Thomas Mantell, died when his F-51 crashed southwest of Franklin, Kentucky—Mantell was chasing a UFO.

The Story:

The infamous Mantell incident, which has been written up in practically every UFO book available, began when several hundred people reported seeing an unusual circular object over Kentucky. The State Police reported it to the Fort Knox Military Police. The MPs, in turn, reported the object to nearby Goodman Air Force Base. The object was sighted as it moved slowly toward the south. Observers say it resembled an ice-cream cone, and watched for nearly ninety minutes as the strange object hung motionless in the sky.

A squadron of F-51s then flew over Goodman AFB. The object was still visible, and the flight commander, Mantell, asked the base if he could

investigate. He proceeded to increase his altitude. The other planes turned back because they were not equipped with oxygen. Mantell reported that the object ahead of him was huge and metallic. He made no further calls, and visual and radio contact was lost as he gained more altitude.

About two hours later, Mantell's plane was found on a farm near Franklin. His watch had stopped at 3:18 P.M. The controls indicated that he had passed out from lack of oxygen at about twenty-five thousand feet, although the plane continued to climb to thirty thousand feet, then leveled out before going into a high-speed dive. The throttle position indicated that Mantell had regained consciousness when the plane reached a lower altitude, and had unsuccessfully tried to slow the plane down and pull out of the dive.

The press picked up on the story immediately and created a national flurry of speculation—namely that a UFO had attacked a U.S. airman because he had gotten too close. The air force came out with several theories. One was that Mantell had been chasing the planet Venus. This was later disproved. They then said that he was pursuing a navy skyhook balloon, which was then top secret. It has never been determined whether or not a skyhook balloon was ever released in the area. Most agree, however, that a lack of oxygen, and not a UFO weapon, was the cause of Mantell's crash.

UFO Watching:
Otter Creek Park, fifteen minutes from Fort Knox, is a wilderness area with cliffs overlooking the Ohio River and a good portion of the Fort Knox area. Call 502-942-3641 for information about the park.

During the Day:
Radcliff/Fort Knox, just forty-five minutes south of Louisville, is the home of the nation's gold depository. You can see the vault—but only from the outside! Take U.S. 31W or Bullion Boulevard leading into Fort Knox. The visitor center is at 306 North Wilson, Radcliff; 800-334-7540.

TAYLORSVILLE LAKE

You'll find Taylorsville at the intersection of Kentucky Highways 44 and 55, about thirty miles southeast of Louisville. Bring your fishing rod and your night-vision binoculars—because both the fish and UFOs are biting.

This area of north-central Kentucky bounded by Taylorsville Lake and Salt River is known, according to reports received by Interlink Kentucky, a UFO research group, for its on-again/off-again sightings. Since August 1998, residents have been reporting seeing a small, very bright, and reddish light in the sky. Its pattern of movement is unpredictable and it appears and disappears suddenly. Small white oval objects have also been witnessed flying in the area.

UFO Watching:

Head to the source of this flap's action. From Louisville, take Interstate 64 to the Gene Snyder Freeway south and Kentucky 155 to Taylorsville. Turn east on Kentucky 44 and drive three miles to the entrance of the town park. Call 502-477-8713 for park information.

Louisiana

....

SHREVEPORT

Shreveport has had a good number of UFO sightings through the years. It's also the location of Barksdale Air Force Base. (Hmmm . . . coincidence?)

The Story:

One notorious incident occurred in September 1975, according to accounts in several encyclopedias and on several research-oriented web sites. Personnel at the base were having a good laugh at a civilian report of a UFO sighting that had come in around midnight. A few minutes later, the guard at the west entrance to the base reported to Command that a UFO was hovering about fifty or sixty feet above the ground. It stayed there for about fifteen minutes, then flew to the south. Soon after, the guards at the nuclear weapons storage area reported that the UFO was hovering over their post. It stayed there for another fifteen to twenty

The late Major Jesse Marcel, the godfather of the famous Roswell, New Mexico, incident lived in Homa, Louisiana.

minutes and then left. Witnesses reported that the object was triangular and about forty feet across. It had dim lights and made no sound as it passed overhead.

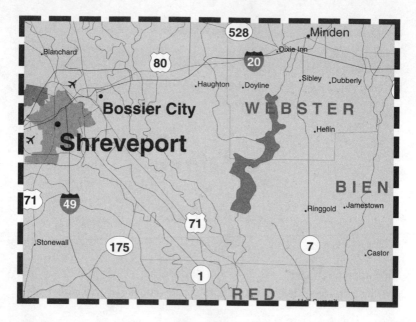

The Site:

Head for **Barksdale Air Force Base** (on Interstate 20), located in Bossier City, Louisiana, next to Shreveport. Call Community Relations, 318-456-5505, for tour information. Barksdale AFB is located in the northwest corner of Louisiana just eighteen miles east of the Texas border and seventy miles south of Arkansas. Interstate 20 goes right by the base, and Interstate 49 ends eight miles from the base.

During the Day:

SPAR Planetarium, 2820 Pershing Blvd., Shreveport, 318-673-STAR. Features multimedia star shows, story telling, school field trips, public shows, private parties, and much more.

Sci-Port Discovery Center, 528 Commerce Street, Downtown Shreveport Riverfront, 318-424-3466, is a hands-on science learning center featuring exciting interactive exhibits and fascinating demonstrations for children and adults of all ages.

Maine

············

ALLAGASH

There is no area in New England that can match the dense, rugged beauty of the Allagash wilderness. It's an outdoor enthusiast's dream vacation. But northern Maine is also a paradise for UFO buffs. This is the sight of hundreds of trails, miles of white water, and two of the most notorious UFO investigations ever documented.

The Story:

This area is the setting for one of the best-documented of all purported mass abduction cases, with its own book called *The Allagash Abductions* by Ray Fowler (the abduction investigator who is now as famous as his most famous cases). It involves four young men who were canoeing along the Allagash Waterway on August 26, 1976. They were in a very remote area, reachable only by plane. All four claim to have experienced missing time, and years later, under hypnosis, they each separately described a detailed and amazingly similar UFO abduction episode. This case is considered unique in the world of UFO research because it provides four separate but consistent and collaborative accounts of the same event.

> *"ONE MUST CONCLUDE THAT THE HIGHLY PUBLICIZED AIR FORCE PRONOUNCEMENTS BASED UPON UNSOUND STATISTICS SERVE MERELY TO MISREPRESENT THE TRUE CHARACTER OF THE UFO PHENOMENA."*
>
> **Yale Scientific Magazine (Yale University) Volume XXXVII, Number 7, April 1963**

It was warm and clear, and you could hear the fish popping up out of the lake, just asking to be caught—the perfect time to do a little night fishing. (Wrong!) Before sliding their canoe into the water, four friends—

Charlie Foltz, Jim Weiner, Chuck Rak, and Jack Weiner—prepared a large bonfire in order to find their way back to camp in the wilderness—black night.

They were halfway across a cove when they supposedly saw a silent, large, brilliant sphere of colored light hovering above the lake about two hundred yards in front of them. One of the men flashed his flashlight at it, and the object moved toward them—and it kept coming. The friends decided to begin paddling back to shore. Their paddling became frantic when the object, they say, emitted a beam of light directly into their canoe.

The next thing Charlie and Jim remembered was standing at the campsite watching the object move back out across the lake. Chuck remembers being in the canoe and watching it disappear. Jack remembers calmly getting out of the canoe.

After the object disappeared, the four walked up the beach to find that the bonfire they had lit just fifteen or twenty minutes earlier had burned down to ash and ember. Jim thought the large logs they had set on the fire should have burned for two to three hours.

Several years later, the men would begin to experience strange dreams of alien abductors. Eventually, they sought the help of well-known UFO investigator Raymond Fowler. Fowler reportedly hypnotized each of the four men separately, and they each told the same tale of being taken aboard the craft and forced to undergo medical examinations by aliens.

UFO Watching:

It's remote. It's dark. It's kind of spooky. Pretty much anywhere you canoe along the **Allagash Wilderness Waterway** (a ninety-two-mile-long protected stretch of lake, shore, and river corridor) is good for sky-viewing.

The longest trip starts at **Telos Lake,** near the northwestern edge of Baxter State Park, and ends at **West Twin Brook.** Many canoeists paddle another five miles to Allagash Village at the confluence of the St. John and Allagash rivers.

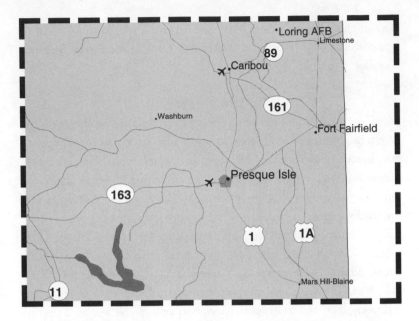

Access to the waterway is limited and restricted in many areas; visitors are encouraged to contact Maine's Bureau of Parks and Lands for canoeing, parking, and registration information (you have to register to travel this area).

Many hiking trails lead to fire towers that offer fine views of the surrounding lakes and woodlands.

For More Information:
Maine Bureau of Parks and Lands, 207-941-4014.

LORING

Are aliens attracted to military installations? Are they just curious about our technology or do they want to assess our defense capabilities? Or, are the sightings simply secret military aircraft? It's a spooky question when you consider what happened at **Maine's Loring Air Force Base** on October 27 and 28, 1975.

The Story:

Personnel guarding the nuclear weapons depot spotted an unknown craft with a bright strobe light coming toward them. The control tower spotted the object on their radar screens. Several attempts were made to communicate with the craft, but no response was received. The craft came very close to the nuclear storage unit, hovered briefly, then shot away at a tremendous speed. The base went on major alert status.

The military notified the North American Aerospace Defense Command (NORAD) (it provides warning of missile and air attack against the United States), but no explanation could be found. The next night at 7:45 P.M., the UFO returned. At one point it appeared 150 feet over the end of a runway, then shut off its lights. It reappeared over the weapons storage area and was seen at close range by a B-52 bomber crew. They described a long, red-and-orange, football-shaped craft, about four car-lengths in size with no visible doors or windows. It vanished when Security Police arrived. The base commander requested air support in case the object returned.

The mysterious craft did not make another appearance—however, strange lights were reported for several weeks afterward in the surrounding towns. You can read about the whole account in exhaustive detail in *The UFO Coverup* by Lawrence Fawcett and Barry J. Greenwood—two well-known UFO/military investigators.

UFO Watching:

Loring Air Force Base located in Aroostook County is now Loring Commerce Center (Limestone, Maine). Limestone is situated at the intersection of three well-maintained highways. Route 89 travels west through downtown Limestone and intersects U.S. Highway 1 at Caribou. U.S.

Highway IA traverses north and south from downtown Limestone. All roads lead to Loring. The skywatching is still good here, it's very wooded and rustic. Fireballs have recently been seen in this area. Head to the **Malabeam Lake Campground** located on the Center's grounds in Limestone, Maine (207-328-4643).

There's also an eighty-five acre **Trafton Lake Recreation Area** located on the Ward Road, three miles from downtown Limestone. It is considered one of the best fishing lakes and who knows what else you might catch?

Maryland

ANNAPOLIS

Just about everyone knows that Annapolis is the home of the Naval Academy. But what most people don't know is that this area along the western shores of the Chesapeake Bay was the sight of a supposed UFO flap in the late 1980s.

The Story:

In April 1988, an Annapolis newspaper reported that at least a dozen residents reported seeing two large and brightly lit UFOs near the Bay Bridge on two separate occasions. The witnesses all claimed that the UFOs hovered in the same spot for more than two hours and that strange electrical things were happening in the sky around the object.

When the sightings were later investigated, it was discovered that the objects had been appearing regularly in a particular neighborhood for weeks. At one point, one of the craft shined a beam of light first on a group of curious onlookers and again at a house. Residents became so

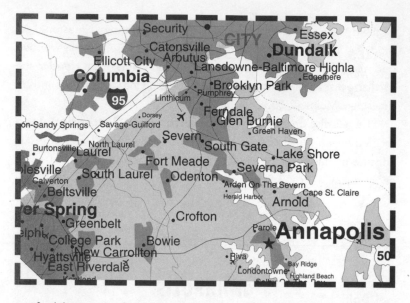

terrified they were afraid to leave their houses at night. Then, as suddenly as it started, the UFO activity ceased and seemed to shift to the other side of the bay into Baltimore.

UFO Watching:

City Dock is located in downtown Annapolis and this waterfront park provides great skywatching. It's located at State Circle and School Street Government House (410-974-3531). **The Chesapeake Bay Bridge** is another good sighting area. Popularly called the Bay Bridge, it's located near Annapolis and crosses the Chesapeake Bay as part of U.S. 50/301. The bridge's dual spans provide a direct connection between Maryland's eastern shore recreational and ocean regions and the metropolitan areas of Baltimore, Annapolis, and Washington, D.C. You obviously can't stop on the bridge to skywatch but you can stop in nearby **Sandy Point State Park,** 1100 East College Parkway, Annapolis, Maryland, for a good view. This was an area that had numerous sightings in the eighties. Call 410-974-2149 for more information about the park.

During the Day:

The U.S. Naval Academy offers a museum and guided tours (Preble Hall, Maryland Avenue). For information, call 410-263-6933. The museum is open Monday to Saturday, from 9 A.M. to 5 P.M. and Sunday from 11 A.M. to 5 P.M.

BALTIMORE

To insiders, Baltimore is known as "Charm City." But on the night of October 26, 1958, the alleged UFO that visited didn't charm residents.

The Story:

The Baltimore-area sightings were documented for MUFON by the well-known investigator Robert Oechsler. One alleged close encounter offers these details: two men were nearing one of the bridges over Loc Haven Dam when they spotted a large, egg-shaped object hanging approximately 150 feet off the top of the superstructure of the bridge. They decided to take a closer look, but their car mysteriously died. The two got out and watched the unusual craft. They alleged that all at once, a bright flash of light heated their faces, and they heard a noise that reminded them of thunder. The craft rose vertically and sped away.

They reported the incident and decided to go to a hospital because their faces felt burned. Several other people also reported seeing what they believed to be the same craft in the same area on the same evening. *The Baltimore Sun* followed the investigation for a while, but ultimately, it was never explained.

UFO Watching:

Head to the **Loc Raven Reservoir** (Dulaney Valley Road off Interstate 695, Towson, MD; 410-887-7691). It's only about ten miles outside of

Baltimore (head north on State Road 45). **Baltimore's Inner Harbor** area on the waterfront is another good skywatching spot (the crabs are good, too).

During the Day:
The Maryland Science Center houses lots of exhibits, and for sky-watchers there's a **Hubble Space Telescope and the Davis Planetarium** (601 Light Street, Baltimore, MD 21230; 410-685-2370).

Located near Baltimore in Greenbelt is a space freak's mecca: **NASA's Goddard Space Flight Center** (Greenbelt Road; 301-286-2000). The Visitor Center is open to the public daily from 9 A.M. to 4 P.M. and closed on Thanksgiving, Christmas, and New Year's Day. There is no admission charge, and parking is free. Public tours include visits to special working areas that show satellite control, spacecraft construction, and communications facilities. There's a gift shop and picnic area.

From Baltimore: Take the Baltimore-Washington Parkway (Route 295) south to the Beltsville Agricultural Research Center. Exit at Powder Mill Road and follow the signs to the Goddard Visitor Center. If you are on official business, continue past the turn for the Visitor Center to the next traffic light (Greenbelt Road). Turn right on Greenbelt Road, then turn right at the next traffic light to enter the main gate.

Massachusetts
••••••••••••

SOUTH ASHBURNHAM

Ashburnham is located in north central Massachusetts, near the New Hampshire border and 55 miles northwest of Boston. One of this city's better-known residents is Betty Andreasson Luca. She is a well-known

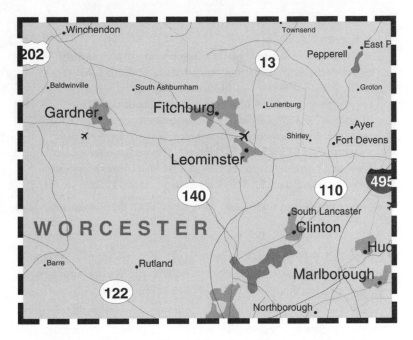

abductee who has gone public with her claim that she is the focus of ongoing abduction experiences. She lectures and writes frequently on her unusual experiences. She believes that the gray aliens she has encountered are bio robots controlled by higher humanlike entities called the Elders. She theorizes that skin samples taken during her abductions are intended for melanin production by the aliens so that they can impersonate humans. The good news is that she believes the intent of alien contact is positive. (This lady is one heck of an optimist.)

The Story:

According to her own account, published in several sources, on the evening of January 25, 1967, Betty Andreasson was in her kitchen. Her family was in the living room. At about 6:30 P.M., the house lights suddenly blinked and then, a pulsating reddish-orange light shined in the kitchen window.

Her father rushed to look out the kitchen window. He purportedly saw a group of strange-looking small creatures approaching with a hopping motion. Five small humanoid creatures entered the house by permeating the wooden door. Betty now believes that her family was placed in suspended animation. The leader of the other four established telepathic communication with Betty—which she claims to maintain on and off to this day (sort of a toll-free number to another planet).

Betty has described the leader as about five feet tall. The others were shorter. Their heads were pear-shaped and they had catlike eyes. Their mouths were slits that didn't move. But Betty's fright was eased by an overpowering sense of friendship. She allowed them to lead her to a small craft that looked like two inverted saucers. Once on board they performed numerous medical exams. She was later returned and could remember only bits and pieces of her experience.

Fearing ridicule, she kept quiet about her experience until 1975 when she saw a local newspaper story about UFO researcher Dr. J. Allen Hynek (no stranger to Massachusetts UFO investigations). She contacted him. A team of experts did extensive interviews with her and performed lie-detector tests and hypnosis sessions. They found her truthful and credible. Their findings are published in a series of books called *The Andreasson Affair.*

UFO Watching:

Allegedly, people near Betty during her abductions have been placed in a state of suspended animation so you won't want to get too close to her house. Instead, head to the nearby **Wapack Trail.** It's a twenty-one-mile ridgeline trail that offers spectacular views from its southern trailhead at the base of Mt. Watatic in Ashburnham, Massachusetts, to the northern slope of North Pack Monadnock in Greenfield, New Hampshire. It is maintained by the Friends of the Wapack (P.O. Box 115, Peterborough, NH 03458), and is marked by yellow triangles. This trail lends itself well to day hikes as it crosses several roads along the way.

Michigan

ANN ARBOR

Early in March 1966, residents around the Ann Arbor area of Michigan were purportedly treated to a spectacular UFO show in their skies. **The wave of 1966** (a "wave" is an ongoing flap or incidence of increased and sustained UFO activity), as it came to be known, was widely publicized across the Unites States after many police officers and public officials weighed in as credible witnesses. It was never proven that any of the UFOs were indeed any kind of alien craft, but the event left a lot of folks in this area wondering.

Folks are still wondering in Dexter, a tiny farm community about 10 miles west of Ann Arbor. This is where the now infamous "swamp gas episode" took place.

The Story:

According to UFO reports from research centers around the country, it all started when a farmer and his son saw something bright fall out of the sky. They found a craftlike object hovering just above a swamp. It flashed red, white, and blue lights. They reported the incident. It is not clear just how many witnesses in addition to the farmer and his son saw the craft over the swamp—however, it is well documented that at the same time, police were chasing similar craftlike objects that had been spotted in Dexter's skies.

According to several sources—including *The Encyclopedia of UFOs*, edited by Ronald D. Story, Allen Hyneck, an astronomy professor and UFO consultant to the Air Force's Project Bluebook, ended up debunking the incident. Hyneck claimed, among other things, that what the witnesses saw could have actually been swamp gas. Though people ridiculed him without mercy, he stuck to his explanation, because swamp gas is known to give off flashing light. The farmer maintains that he had seen swamp gas before and that was not what he had seen that night. And it didn't explain the objects that hundreds of others had seen in the skies (not over the swamps) during this time.

> **SWAMP GAS: A DEFINITION**
> It has no smell, but makes small popping explosions.
> The gas forms from decomposition of vegetation and is
> made up of methane, hydrogen sulfide, and phosphine. It
> gives off a light that resembles flames that appear in one
> place, disappear, and then appear in another. Its colors
> are often yellow, red, or blue-green.

Hyneck's swamp gas explanation was ironic considering that he was one of the earliest proponents of UFO investigation. This case represents a turning of the tide in military-civilian UFO relations. The public suddenly felt that the government was not really interested in finding, or revealing, the truth. However, immediately after these incidents, Gerald Ford, then House Republican Leader, called for a UFO investigation.

UFO Watching:

Located on the Huron River Drive at Barton Lane Drive across from Bird Hills Park, **Barton Park** is a good place for skywatching. The park's phone number is 734-994-2780.

Swamp Gas Hunting:

Located just ten minutes west of Ann Arbor, take Interstate 94 and exit at Baker Road, and you are in swamp gas country. To get to the general vicinity of the original swamp gas episode, turn right onto Baker Road, and make a left onto Main Street which becomes Dexter Pinckney Road. From there go straight and you will pick up Island Lake Road. Turn right onto Dexter Townhall Road, then right onto Fleming Road, then left onto McGuiness.

Unfortunately swamps aren't listed on maps and many are on private property, so you are at the mercy of your personality for getting one of the local farmers to let you on his or her land. If all else fails, head to the **Timberland Campground,** 12780 North Territorial in Dexter

(734-475-8679). There are thirty lakes within a fifteen-mile radius of Dexter and the Huron River flows through the edge of town. All of this water makes for good skywatching along any shore and lots of gas in the air.

FLINT

On Friday, March 17, 1995 the National UFO Reporting Center Hotline received an interesting report from an FAA air traffic controller near Flint, Michigan. The controller claimed that he and four other controllers had been witness to a sighting of strange objects flying near their tower.

The Story:

They allegedly saw four bright red, pulsating objects. The controller reported that it looked somewhat like a "red road flare," although they said it pulsated at regular intervals. Moreover, in the midst of each pulsation, when the radiated light subsided, an object appeared to be visible within the "cloud" of red light. It appeared to be a different shape after each pulse.

The controller reported that one member of the group flashed the tower's light "gun" at the nearest of the four objects, at which point the object instantly returned to the shape and size of a small "fireball," and began darting and zigzagging in the evening sky. None of the objects appeared on the radar screen in the tower.

On March 23, the same group of controllers reported another sighting from their tower. During this third sighting, even the tower supervisors were witnesses to the objects.

UFO Watching:

For reasons that are as unexplainable as UFOs, ballooning is a big hobby in Flint, and it's a great way to get closer to other worlds and watch the sky up close. Just stay away from that control tower! Contact **Balloon Quest/Captain Phogg Balloon Rides,** 248-634-3094.

During the Day:

Michigan's largest planetarium, the **Longway Planetarium,** is located in Flint and has a renowned laser show. Its address and phone number are 1310 East Kearsley Street; 810-760-1181. Star shows are Saturdays and Sundays at 1 and 2:30 P.M. Laser shows are Friday and Saturday evenings.

Minnesota
....

MINNEAPOLIS/ST. PAUL

It's not true that Minnesota is the land of ten thousand lakes. It's actually home to 11,842 of them—and weird things are said to hover over the waters here.

New Brighton, a suburb located seven miles north of downtown Minneapolis, has also been the scene of on-and-off UFO activity. There was a miniflap here in 1997 around Long Lake Road, with numerous triangular crafts spotted in the skies. The same crafts were also seen traveling at breakneck speeds along Interstate Highways 694 and 35W.

Investigators theorized that the **U.S. Army's Twin Cities Ammunition Plant** in Arden Hills, Minnesota, just across Long Lake from New Brighton, could be a possible site of interest for UFOs.

UFO Watching:

For some serious skywatching, head to the **Foshay Tower** on 821 Marquette Avenue in Minneapolis (612-359-3030), a historic landmark that provides the only outdoor observation deck in the Twin Cities.

Also try **Highways 694** and **35 West** just outside of town and the Long Lake Road in town.

During the Day:
The Minneapolis Planetarium, (300 Nicollet Mall, Minneapolis, MN 55401; 612-630-6150) offers the usual fare.

For More Information:
<u>**Saint Paul Convention and Visitors Bureau,**</u>
651-265-4900 or 800-627-6101.
<u>**Minneapolis Convention and Visitors Association,**</u> **612-348-7000.**

STEPHEN

Looking for a hot time in an old town? Travel just seventy-two miles outside of the capital city of St. Paul to the tiny town of Stephen and ask any of its six hundred residents about the famous **Stephen Fireball** that once attacked a police officer.

The Story:

They'll tell you that on August 27, 1979, Deputy Val Johnson of Marshall County was on a routine patrol ten miles west of the city when he saw an unusual light in the sky. First he thought it might be an airplane, but then the light shot forward directly at his car. The next thing he knew, he was engulfed in a blinding flash of light and heard glass breaking. His car crashed and he lost consciousness. When he awoke, he was suffering from severe soreness in his eyes and had mild burns from exposure to intense light.

The officer who investigated the crash scene noted considerable damage to Johnson's vehicle, but could not account for it. It was also discovered that the car clock and Johnson's watch agreed with each other, but were both fourteen minutes slow. This case was subsequently investigated by the Center for UFO Studies which published a report about it, but no one knows what happened, and Johnson cannot recall what happened after the light blinded him. This spooky case remains unsolved.

The Site:

From the center of town, travel about ten miles west on **Highway 220.** This is the general spot where Johnson crashed. There have been other sightings in this area. (Bring sunglasses.)

For More Information:

East Grand Forks Chamber of Commerce, 218-773-7481.

Mississippi

••••••••••••

PASCAGOULA/GAUTIER

The Gulf Coast of Mississippi is considered the "Playground of the South." There are twenty-six miles of beaches and a casino-filled nightlife. And while you sit and watch the sun dip out of the sky, here's a twisted tale to think about—the alleged abduction of two men on October 11, 1973.

The Story:

It's considered the second most famous abduction case on record (the first being New Hampshire's Hill case). It received enormous publicity—probably due to the fact that it was reported at the onset of the great American UFO wave that erupted that month.

According to numerous accounts of this famous case, including UFO researcher's Jerome Clark's account as it appears in *The UFO Book,* the men were fishing from a dock along the Pascagoula River when they heard a buzzing noise behind them. They turned to see what they claim was a domed, football-shaped object approximately thirty feet long and ten feet high hovering above the riverbank. They watched in horror as a door opened and three beings floated out toward them. The aliens were allegedly about five feet tall, had bullet-shaped heads, and no necks. They had long arms, claw like hands, and legs that didn't separate.

Two of the beings allegedly seized one of the men, who felt a stinging sensation and then became paralyzed. The third being held the other man, who had fainted from fright. They recalled being taken into the craft where both men were suspended in the air while a huge electronic eye came out of the wall and examined them.

Twenty minutes later, the men were ejected onto the ground. The object rose straight up and sped out of sight. Their experience eventually

made it onto the wire services, who reported the incident. Investigators who interviewed the witnesses believed the men were being truthful, and both men passed lie detector tests.

UFO Watching:

The Mississippi Gulf Coast hugs the Gulf of Mexico and is approximately an hour's drive from New Orleans, Louisiana, to the west and Mobile, Alabama, to the east. Head to City Park Pier—at the foot of Beach Boulevard. This is a public fishing pier and provides great views of the river and sky. Any of the Mississippi beaches are going to give you an awesome sky view. (Just remember to look behind you!)

During the Day:

It's worth the trip to the **Stennis Space Center** (SSC) just to see the billions-and-billions-year-old moon rock. Stennis is its own town and is comprised of the Center's large campus. It's located in the southwest corner of Mississippi, about fifty miles northeast of New Orleans, Louisiana, and thirty miles from the Mississippi Gulf Coast. Visitor Center hours are 9 A.M. to 4 P.M., Monday through Saturday, and noon to 4 P.M. on Sunday.

The Center is located on State Highway 607 with easy access from Interstate 10. (From the Gulf Coast head west.) Signs are located along the roadways with directions to the Space Center and the Visitors Center (228-688-2370).

Missouri
·············

JOPLIN

"Well now it goes through St. Lou-ee/Jop-lin Mi-ssou-ree," sings Bobby Troop in his 1946 hit "Route 66," the song that put this town on the map. But Joplin is famous for something else—the alleged enigma of the **"Hornet Spook Light"** (HSL). The appearance of these lights can be traced to Indian legend. They've been attracting tourists long before the construction of U.S. Route 66.

The Story:

This unusual phenomenon along a stretch of road called **Devil's Promenade** on **BB Highway** (a county highway so small it doesn't even get a number) has been attributed to everything from ghosts to natural light refractions to UFO trace matter. Some people think that the light is the ghost of an Osage chief who was murdered near this spot. No matter what it is, everyone agrees that the colored lights which spontaneously appear and bob around are indeed spooky.

The lights are unpredictable, changing color and shape with every movement. Sometimes they allegedly hop over cars and nearby fields, and if you get close to them, they vanish. Distant sightings of and close encounters with the HSL continue to be reported.

The Site:

To see the lights with your own eyes, take Interstate 44 west from Joplin to Highway 43. Drive south on 43 approximately six miles to BB Highway. Turn right. Drive about three miles to the road's end. Turn right and drive another mile to a second dirt road to the left. You will see the old "Spookies" building on the right (it's an old museum and the only building around). You will now be headed west on "Spook Light Road." The road is long but travel to a dark point about one-and-a-half miles down. Park anywhere and wait. You can even see them from your car. Some witnesses have reported the lights coming up and bouncing off their hoods.

For More Information:
City of Joplin Tourism Center, 800-657-2534.

Montana
· · · · · · · · · · · ·
GREAT FALLS

Great Falls lies in the heart of Big Sky Country amidst the Glacier-Waterton International Peace Park. The Rocky Mountains are to its west and Little Belt Mountains to the east. The city was settled around the Missouri River, which provided Great Falls with its name and its waterfalls. The scenery here is drop-dead gorgeous.

There's also a lot of UFO history here. One of the strongest cases supporting the existence of UFOs allegedly occurred here in August 1950.

The Story:
The then-general-manager of the Great Falls Selectrics baseball team reported seeing two rotating disk-shaped objects zipping around in the

sky and captured it on sixteen-millimeter colored movie film. This film has been heavily analyzed, and has stood the tough tests of debunkers. It eventually ended up in the hands of air force investigators who said they were jets flying in the area. However, the manager says that he had seen the jets they referred to earlier in another part of the sky, and that he hadn't captured the jets on film.

Great Falls is also home to the **Malmstrom Air Force Base,** one of the most infamous military spots for supposed UFO activities.

Numerous UFO sightings have been reported in the area, and some notorious incidents took place here. According to many sources, including *Above Top Secret* by Timothy Good and *The UFO Coverup* by Lawrence Fawcett and Barry J. Greenwood, on November 7, 1975, remote electronic sensors at the base (home to more than twenty Minuteman missiles) indicated that something had violated base security. A sabotage alert team (big guys in black uniforms with big guns) was dispatched by helicopter to investigate, and as the team approached, they supposedly saw an orange, football-shaped object. They were ordered to get closer but they refused. The object was later picked up on radar by NORAD, and two F-106 jets were launched. As the jets approached, the object shot away and was lost from radar. Supposedly operators at the launch control facility later discovered that the missiles had all had their target coordinates tampered with.

The Site:

Tours of the **air force base** are available on a walk-in basis every other Friday at the Malmstrom Visitors' Center but they have to have your request in writing at least a week prior: 7015 Goddard Drive, Room 167, Malmstrom AFB, Great Falls, MO 59402-6863. For more information, call 406-731-4050.

UFO Watching:

Get in shape while you hunt for UFOs. Great Falls has the **River's Edge Trail**—an eleven-mile trail spanning across Great Falls along the Missouri River. It combines fitness (you will meet walkers, runners, skaters, and bikers) with wonderful sky and water vistas. The trail begins at Odd Fellows Park near the Sun River confluence with the Missouri River and ends just east of Cochrane Dam (the pavement stops at the Lewis and Clark Overlook/trailhead, Rainbow Falls). **Glacier National Park** has great sky-viewing areas and camping facilities. Call 800-436-7275 for campground reservations.

Nebraska

· · · · · · · · · · · ·

ASHLAND

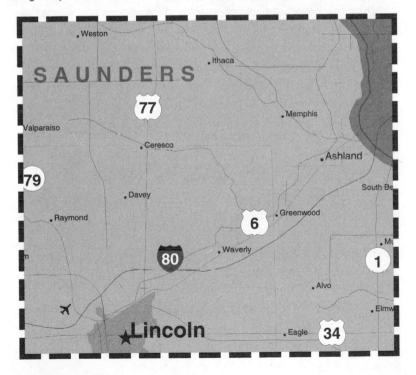

Nebraska's most famous close encounter allegedly happened here in the small town of Ashland about thirty miles from Omaha.

The Story:

It was December 3, 1967 and according to several accounts that include CNI News, a patrolman was on routine late-night patrol at the junction of Highways 6 and 63. He noticed a group of lights ahead of him. When he neared, he allegedly saw a football-shaped UFO suddenly take off. He went home that morning with a splitting headache, an inexplicable red welt on the side of his neck, and about twenty minutes of time he couldn't account for.

The Condon Committee was in the midst of its UFO study at that time, and heard about the patrolman. They suggested that he undergo hypnotic regression to see if he could remember more details of the incident. Under hypnosis, a startling story emerged.

The patrolman supposedly recalled under hypnosis that a lighted object came toward him and landed near his car. Several beings (who looked humanoid, but were definitely not human) emerged. Without knowing why, he rolled down his window. The beings he described had grayish white skin, narrow heads, and their mouths were slits that didn't move. He reported that they wore silver jumpsuits with the emblem of a winged serpent on it. They allegedly took him to the spacecraft. The beings supposedly communicated both audibly and telepathically with the police officer—they told him that they had been watching the human race for a long time and were engaged in a breeding analysis program. The patrolman states that he didn't feel their intent toward him was hostile. Before they let him go they told him they would visit him again. And you thought your relatives were pesky visitors!

The Site:

Ashland is located approximately twenty-five miles southwest of Omaha or twenty-five miles northeast of Lincoln on U.S. Highway 6. Highway 6 connects with Interstate 80 five miles south and seven miles north of Ashland. Head to the spot where the officer claims he was abducted at the junction of Highways 6 and 63 outside of Ashland.

UFO Watching:

The **Eugene T. Mahoney State Park** (28500 West Park Highway Ashland, NE 68003; 402-944-2523) is another good skywatching spot.

The park overlooks the valley of the Platte River near Ashland. It's located on I-80. If heights don't freak you out, look for signs for the seventy-foot-tall **Walter Scott Jr. Observation Tower** located in the park.

During the Day:

Adjacent to the park, you will conveniently find the **Strategic Air Command Museum.** (It's also accessible from Interstate 80 at the Mahoney State Park exit; 402-944-3100). The **SAC Museum** has thirty-three aircraft and six missiles that are on display. The new museum has a restoration and preservation gallery for ongoing work on aircraft. It's open daily from 9 A.M. to 6 P.M.; admission is $6.00 for adults and $3.00 for children ages five to twelve.

Nevada
....

RACHEL/AREA 51

Welcome to the **UFO capital of the United States**—and possibly even the world. Area 51, also known as **Groom Lake,** is a supposedly top secret military facility about ninety miles north of Las Vegas. Within the area—which spans several miles—is allegedly a secret air base the government has been operating since the 1950s. Groom Lake (a dry lakebed used for aircraft landings) is known to be a testing ground for military aircraft before they are publicly acknowledged.

The Story:

In 1989 the facility became notorious for UFO conspiracy and cover-up when a highly credible scientist named Bob Lazar publicly claimed to have worked with an alien spacecraft in an area just south of Area 51. He

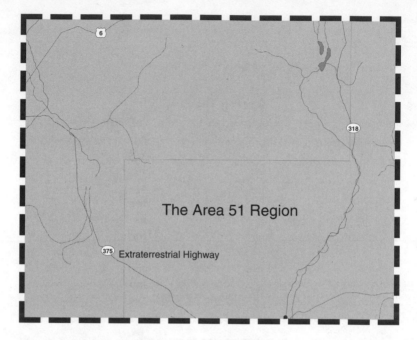

The Area 51 Region

375 Extraterrestrial Highway

also claimed that he had seen alien saucers flying around Highway 375 near Rachel. Thus, the legend was born, and soon people from all over were parked along this remote highway trying to have a close encounter of any kind.

Rachel is the closest thing to a town near Area 51, but you could spit and if the wind were right, you would get the whole town wet. There's a local bar, a gas station, and a convenience store, and that's about it—except for the alleged UFOs. Many visitors are convinced that the U.S. government is testing alien spacecraft just beyond the mountains that overlook this tiny desert town. Many believe that the government may be trying to analyze alien technology in order to further our own technological and military capabilities. No one is sure what the military is testing here, but visitors usually see a lot of sky action. You can expect to see jets dogfighting, flares going off, and strange lights, and you'll probably hear a sonic boom that will rattle your bones—this is not a dull place.

UFO RADIO TODAY

"From the high desert and the great American Southwest this is Art Bell."

If UFO believers, conspiracy theorists, and millions of insomniacs have one thing in common, it's **Art Bell**. Even people who don't believe in UFOs and the paranormal tune into Art's late night radio show, which he airs, single-handedly, from his home in Parumph, Nevada (about 60 miles outside of Las Vegas).

Just who is this guy? That is as difficult to answer as it is to classify his curious eclectic show which blends current events, science, and the paranormal into one big entertaining and informative soup of ideas. Where else can you hear live guests and callers discuss an update on the Dow Jones, ponder possible alien autopsy cover-ups, learn about the discovery of new distant Quasars, relive a shark attack, and explore the topic of spontaneous human combustion?

Although mostly conservative, Art has more moderate views on some issues, and he holds little back. His fans appreciate his no-nonsense attitude but know that this is no ordinary talk show mortal. According to his biography found on his extensive web site, by the age of 13, Art was a news junkie FCC-licensed radio technician. A few years later, as a young airman, he and a friend built a bootleg radio station on Amarillo Air Force base and secretly broadcast rock and roll music. As a civilian DJ, Art made *The Guinness Book of World Records* for a 116 hour (and 15 minutes) solo broadcast marathon. He later chartered a plane to Vietnam and rescued Vietnamese orphans stranded in Saigon after the war.

Art has been doing his Coast to Coast (weeknights 10 P.M., 9 to 3 A.M. PST) show, "Dreamland," for over 14 years now, and is still growing in popularity, as evident by the now 400 plus stations that carry his nightly show.

(continued on page 110)

(continued from page 109)

Just how popular this unusual radio host is became clear by thenationwide media frenzy that ensued after his abrupt and mysterious departure on October 12, 1998 from the airwaves. Virtually every network was camped on his front lawn to find out why; to the shock and worry of his fans, he announced that his career was over and he was signing off the air due to a grave family situation. Fortunately, Art returned two weeks later and told his listeners that a threat to his son's safety had been the cause of his hasty departure. (Art's son is apparently okay). The whole story, Art promised, will one day be told.

To get in touch with Art if you have a question, UFO report, or comment, you can reach him by e-mail at artbell@aol.com, but be warned—his box on AOL fills up many times a day. You can also write him at Art Bell, PO Box 4755, Pahrump, NV 89041-4755, or fax him at 702-727-8499.

To tune into Art's show on the road, call 541-664-8829 to find out his affiliates.

The Sites:

Rachel is located about twenty miles from Area 51 and two hours from Las Vegas on Highway 375, which was officially renamed by the state of Nevada **"the Extraterrestrial Highway."**

Two loop tours are possible: From Las Vegas, take Interstate 15 and U.S. 93 to the ET Highway, then return via U.S. Highways 6 and 95. From Reno, take Interstate 80 to Alternate U.S. Highway 50. Go south on U.S. 95 to U.S. 6, then east to the ET Highway. Return the same way or extend your trip down to Las Vegas and back up via U.S. Highway 95. Depending on route choice and pace, the loop tour takes two to six days. You can do a day trip from Las Vegas.

The junction of 318 (north) and 375 (north) near Alamo, Nevada is where the first ET sign is located. You can't get inside the facility located there, and don't try. Your best bet is to contact Out There Tours (see below if you want the inside scoop on what's really happening and how to find it).

You might have read about the **Little A'Le'Inn** (pronounced "Little Alien") in *USA Today*. This is Rachel's only restaurant, bar, and motel. It's ground zero for UFO visitors (HCR Box 45, Rachel, NV 89001; 702-729-2515). The small statue you see outside is a time capsule and monument for the 1996 movie *Independence Day*.

The **Area 51 Research Center** (also known as Ufomind, located on the ET Highway, 775-729-2648) is a private company that investigates UFO claims. They maintain the world's largest paranormal web site (www.ufomind.com). They also have a retail store that mostly features books. You can literally find everything you could ever want to know about Area 51 here—it's run by Glenn Campbell (no relation to the country singer), who is considered the leading authority on this subject. On the ET Highway, look for the yellow trailer with the "Area 51 Research Center" sign. You're there!

Used in the late 1960s to train astronauts for the Apollo moon mission, **Lunar Crater Volcanic Field** covers more than one hundred square miles, and contains cinder cones, lava flows, and craters. The unusual landscape was formed when molten lava surfaced along a fault line in the earth's crust. Violent eruptions created Easy Chair Crater and Lunar Crater. The field is located on federal land in the Pancake Mountain Range of Nye County, twenty-eight miles east of the junction of the ET Highway and U.S. Highway 6. It's about 90 miles from Rachel and it's even less populated. You can't even find a gas station around here so bring a full tank, extra drinking water, and food.

Tours:

Out There Tours, 702-594-9885, offers guided tours of many of the ET Highway sites.

For More Information:

Rachel/Area 51 Visitor's Guide,
800-638-2328.

New Hampshire

············

EXETER

One of the best-documented UFO accounts on record allegedly took place during a flap in this small New England community famous for its prestigious academy. More than sixty sightings have been reported from this single location. This also became the subject of a popular book, *Incident at Exeter* by John G. Fuller.

The Story:

A patrolman was riding on Route 101 just outside of Exeter when he came upon a woman just sitting in her car. He asked her if she needed help. She said that a UFO had just chased her car from Epping to Exeter. She said it was large, elliptical in shape, and had red glowing lights. Though the officer saw a bright light on the horizon, he didn't take her report seriously.

Then he received another UFO report. A man had been hitchhiking from Amesbury, Massachusetts, back to Exeter when he saw a large, round object carrying four bright red lights. The supposed object rose out of the woods and hovered over a nearby farmhouse. When the patrolman and the hitchhiker returned to the scene, they saw nothing—at first. Then, allegedly, the same object silently and suddenly rose from behind some trees. The two ran back to the car and waited until it flew away.

The Site:

The first sighting took place on the **Route 101 bypass,** just outside of Exeter. Drive from Epping to Exeter on Route 101. The second sighting was at **a farm on Route 150** in Kensington, New Hampshire, which is a few miles outside of Exeter. The UFO was allegedly seen near an open field bordering the road. Look for **telephone pole #668** for the site of that incident.

PORTSMOUTH

One of the first ever reported abduction cases happened to a couple in this New Hampshire community—it's well documented and has been written about in just about all of the alien abduction and UFO literature as well as in the mainstream press. Paul Fuller wrote a best-selling book about their supposed experience called *The Interrupted Journey*. A movie called *The UFO Incident* was also made about the alleged abduction. The wife, Betty Hill, still lectures about her alleged abduction to this day.

The Story:

In September 1961, the couple was driving back to Portsmouth from a vacation in Canada through New Hampshire's White Mountains. The road was deserted, but they allegedly noticed a light that seemed to be following their car. They thought it was an airplane, helicopter, or meteorite. When it came closer, they stopped the car and the husband looked at it through his binoculars. He later described seeing a coin-shaped craft with blue lighted windows along the edge. He was supposedly able to see into the craft, and observed small figures in it. He thought that he simply got back into the car and drove home to Portsmouth.

However, when they arrived home, they realized that they were two hours late and didn't know why. There were also unusual marks on their car, scuffs on their shoes, and strange stains and tears on Betty's dress.

The wife reported the incident to Pease Air Force Base, and base officials confirmed that they had indeed been tracking an unknown object around that time and location. Soon afterward, according to a doctor who hypnotized the couple, they began to have headaches and nightmares. The doctor was amazed that each described being taken against their will onto a UFO and having medical tests performed on them. The wife remembered that the aliens gave her a pregnancy test, and seemed to be fascinated with her husband's dentures.

She also remembered being shown a "star map" of where the aliens said they came from. Under further hypnotic sessions the couple was supposedly able to re-create the star map, which turned out to closely match a known star system.

Their story became a sensation in 1966, when *Look* magazine made it the centerpiece of a special two-issue report. Critics claim that the alleged abduction was merely a case of hypnotic suggestion.

The Site:

The exact location where the couple was abducted is not exactly known, although the incident allegedly occurred somewhere on **Route 3** near the small town of Groveton. It's located in Coos County, at the junction of U.S. Route 3 and State Route 110.

UFO Watching:

Portsmouth is located on New England's gorgeous seacoast, with the Maine border to its north and the greater Boston area to the south. Try viewing from **Prescott Park,** on Marcy Street at the edge of the Piscataqua River and across from Strawberry Banke Museum.

The old **Pease Air Force Base,** just outside Portsmouth, is also regarded as an especially hot UFO spot, although it closed several years ago. It's now an industrial sight called the Pease International Tradeport (360 Corporate Drive, Portsmouth; 603-334-6031) with an airport.

From Boston: Take Interstate 95 north into New Hampshire, continuing through the Hampton tolls toward Portsmouth. As you pass Exit 3 for Route 101/Greenland, move into the left-hand (passing) lane. Stay in the left-hand lane for Route 4/Spaulding Turnpike. Approximately two miles from the split, take Exit 1 on the right and turn left at the bottom of the ramp for Pease International Tradeport.

New Jersey

•••••••••••

GROVER'S MILL

"Ladies and gentlemen, I have just been handed a message that came in from Grover's Mill by telephone....Just a moment....At least forty people, including six state troopers, lie dead in a field east of the village of Grover's

Mill, their bodies burned and distorted beyond all recognition. . . . "

On October 30, 1938, Orson Welles and his newly formed Mercury Theater group broadcast their radio adaptation of H.G. Wells's *War of the Worlds*. At 8 P.M. that Sunday evening, with programming interrupted with "news bulletins," about twelve million people heard that martians had begun an invasion of Earth in an out-of-the-way place called Grover's Mill, New Jersey. An estimated one million people believed that what they were hearing was true.

The "Panic Broadcast," as it came to be known, sent terrified residents from all over the country screaming into the street. During the broadcast, emergency instructions were given reinforcing everyone's belief of impending doom.

The Site:
Grover's Mill is located in West Windsor Township near Princeton, New Jersey. The **"War of the Worlds" monument,** which depicts a family listening to a radio while a flying saucer lands, is located in Van Nest Park on Cranberry Road in West Windsor. Souvenirs can be purchased from **Ellsworth Wines and Liquors** on Route 571 and Cranberry Road, and **McCaffrey's Market** on Cranberry Road.

For More Information:
NJ Tourism Information, 800-JERSEY7.

WRIGHTSTOWN/McGUIRE AIR FORCE BASE

There have been frequent sightings reported over this busy base area for many years. Locals claim it's still a good spot for sightings (though officials at the base deny this). Back in 1978, according to an account given in the book *An Alien Harvest* by the well-known UFO/cattle mutilation researcher

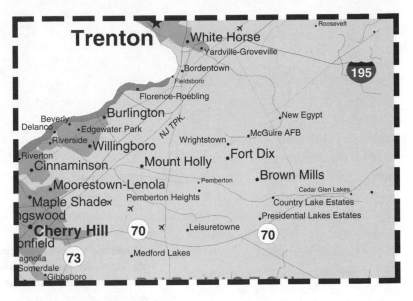

Linda Moulton Howe, an alien allegedly crashed in the area and was shot, killed, and shipped off by military personnel here.

THE SITE:

To get to the base, from New Jersey Turnpike take Exit 7 or from Interstate 295, take the McGuire/Fort Dix exit. Then take U.S. Route 206 south for approximately half a mile. Stay in the left lane to the "Y" intersection of Routes 206 and 68. Turn left on Route 68 and go approximately four miles. Look for a sign pointing left to "McGuire/Deborah Hospital." Turn left at the sign and cross the opposite lanes of Route 68. At the immediate "T" intersection, turn right on Burlington County Route 545 and head south for approximately two miles (crossing Burlington County Route 537 at the one-and-a-half-mile point). At the intersection of Route 537, continue straight ahead as the road becomes a four-lane, divided highway. Follow the four-lane highway (which becomes Burlington County Route 680) straight into McGuire Air Force Base, Gate 2. If Gate 2 is closed, turn left and proceed one quarter of a mile to Gate 1 (twenty-four-hour gate) on your right.

New Mexico

·············

ROSWELL

Will Rogers once called Roswell, New Mexico "the prettiest little town in the West." Years later his observation holds up. Roswell is still a pretty town, boasting startling blue skies and some of the richest ranch land in the country. And with a population of just about fifty thousand, it's still little. Although to update Rogers's description of the town, you would have to add: "and the **UFO crash capital of the United States.**"

Factoid: Demi Moore was born in Roswell but claims to have heard nothing about the crash while growing up. Sounds like a cover-up.

That would explain why the town's highlights include not only two dozen parks and recreational facilities, a local theater company, and a flying school, but a UFO museum as well. What else would you expect from the alleged site of a world-famous UFO crash, a rumored military cover-up, and a possible alien autopsy? To be sure, this pretty little town makes for one heck of an interesting place to visit.

The Story:

Here's the scoop according to dozens of sources, including a June 1997 *Time* magazine cover story: On June 14, 1947, while making routine rounds on the J.B. Foster sheep ranch, eight-five miles northwest of Roswell, rancher Mac Brazel allegedly discovered some litter in a pasture: rubber strips, tinfoil, Scotch tape, and wood. He also claimed to have found very thin metallic slices that couldn't be cut with a knife or burned with matches.

Unbeknownst to Brazel (who had no radio in his ranch shack) there had been a rash of flying saucer reports from all over the country around

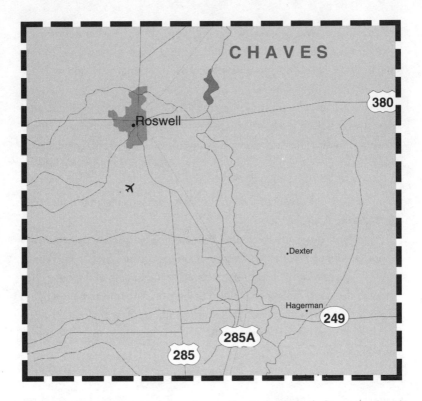

the time of his discovery. According to the *Roswell Daily Record,* a local couple reported seeing a large object zoom across the sky at high speed, possibly four to five hundred miles per hour. The couple reported that the object was oval in shape and glowed as though a light was showing through from the inside.

When Brazel finally learned of the UFO sightings, he wondered if there might be some connection and took some of the debris he had found to the county sheriff in Roswell, who then turned it over to officials at the Roswell Army Air Force Base.

The next day, Brazel led two army intelligence officers to the ranch field where the debris was scattered. They picked up a number of pieces and headed back to town. On the way back to the base, one of the intelligence officers, Major Jesse A. Marcel, stopped to show the debris to his wife and son—the son now remembers that there were pieces of foil, chunks of a Bakelite-looking plastic, and a light I-beam inscribed with purple hieroglyph like symbols.

Major Marcel then took the debris to the base commander who almost immediately issued a press release. The Associated Press announcement, published worldwide on July 8, 1947, from Colonel Blanchard, Base Commander at Roswell Army Air Field, stated: "We have in our possession a flying saucer."

The town of Roswell and the national media was instantly captivated by the news. A furor ensued.

The next day, however, the statement was quickly retracted by Brigadier General Roger M. Ramey of the Eighth Air Force in Ft. Worth, Texas—where Marcel had been ordered to take some of the debris for analysis. General Ramey explained to the press that the so-called flying saucer was nothing more than an experimental weather balloon. The official story ended here. But the unofficial story continued to unfold and is still unfolding to this day:

The infamous Ragsdale crash site.

Glenn Dennis, a mortician in Roswell at the time of the crash, now the cofounder of the UFO Museum there, steadfastly maintains that on July 7, 1947 he received two strange phone calls from a man who claimed to be a mortuary officer. He first asked if Dennis had any hermetically sealed baby caskets in stock. Then he called back to ask what embalming fluids would do to a body.

Factoid: *The nation's largest mozzarella plant is located in Roswell— coincidence?*

Even more interesting is Dennis's claim that he had seen strange activity at the hospital early in July and had been ordered to leave after encountering a hysterical army nurse who eventually told him that she had aided doctors performing autopsies on strange-looking, small bodies. The nurse, he later learned, was killed in a plane crash.

In 1997, under growing pressure from the UFO community, government authorities reinvestigated the Roswell affair. The authorities have since reaffirmed that nothing more than an experimental weather balloon crashed that day in 1947. They also reconfirmed that the rumored dead aliens were, in fact, test dummies dropped from high altitude balloons by the air force. Go forth and decide for yourself.

The Sites:

The Brazel House and Sheep Pasture is seventy miles northwest of Roswell off Interstate 42. This is ground zero in the Roswell incident—the place where Bazel allegedly found the mysterious debris. There's not much to look at now but sheep, although some people claim to feel "unusual" vibes or some kind of energy from the ground.

Hub Corn's ranch is thirty miles north of Roswell off Interstate 285. Were there two crash sites? Explore this twenty-four-square-mile sheep ranch, reputedly the site of an additional 1947 UFO crash. Many authors, historians, and event survivors claim that this is the actual final resting place of the flying saucer and its alien passengers. Monuments have been erected in honor of those aliens that lost their lives there.

Ragsdale's campsite is located fifty miles west of Roswell on Pine Lodge Road, and the Ragsdale crash site is located at the base of the Capitan Mountains. James "Jim" Ragsdale claims that on July 4, 1997, he and his girlfriend not only witnessed a flying saucer crash but that they also saw the bodies of the mysterious "little people" inside. Many argue that it would have been unlikely, if not impossible, for such a loud crash not to have been heard by those at nearby Pine Lodge. Nevertheless, a seven-by-ten-foot rock at the site was visibly split in two.

During the Day:

International UFO Museum and Research Center, 114 North Main Street (Monday to Saturday, from 11 A.M. to 5 P.M., admission free; 505-625-9495). This small but worthy museum housed in an old movie theater offers an illuminating look at UFO phenomena in general and Roswell in particular. Take extra cash to blow in the great gift shop and be sure to slide up to the Alien Caffeine Espresso Bar. A great place to meet illegal aliens.

The Robert H. Goddard Planetarium is located at the Roswell Museum and Art Center, 100 West Eleventh Street. There are public shows one week per month—Tuesday through Saturday at 1:30 P.M. and Friday evenings at 7:30 P.M. General admission is $2.00 and for museum members, $1.00. Laser Light Shows are $5.00. Call 505-624-6744 for more information.

Star Child (108 West First Street, 505-627-6990) is a hip alien gift shop. Bring plenty of Martian Money, and save room in your suitcase for the "I was abducted by aliens and all I got was this stupid T-shirt" T-shirt.

Shopper's Hint: The most popular gift trinket in Roswell is the Alien Head Whistle for $9.00

Tours:

Crash Site Tours, run by Bruce Rhodes, offers tours of two of the crash sites—the main debris site and the Ragsdale site. Call him at 505-622-0628, and plan for a full day's trip. Rates vary.

SOCORRO

Socorro is a small town located about an hour south of Albuquerque, New Mexico. You would think that like the town of Roswell, folks in this town would have capitalized on their UFO fame, but it didn't stick. Ironically, many feel that the infamous Socorro case supplies much more evidence of actual alien activity than the Roswell incident. Today, Socorro is an odd mix of fast food restaurants and old historic buildings with dignity and charm. Some say it has a ghost town feeling to it.

The Story:

This alleged incident has been written about extensively in just about every UFO-related book out there. Government papers on the case were also made available to the public through the Freedom of Information Act. Here's a short version: On April 24, 1964, a police officer had just dropped his pursuit of a speeding car to go check on reports of an explosion on the outskirts of town. He allegedly saw a metallic object in a gully by the road. He got out of his car and saw what he later described as an alien craft—an elongated, oval-shaped object on supporting legs—and two small, humanoid like aliens. Then he heard a noise, like a roar, that startled him—the object rose up and took off. Where the object had been, he allegedly saw a half-burned bush, four angular impressions in the sandy soil (where the legs of the craft might have been), and several small footprints and other impressions.

The Socorro incident is important in UFO history because it was the first instance of an alien sighting, which was not immediately dismissed or discredited by the U.S. Air Force. Perhaps it was the credible witness, or the media blitz which surrounded the event. The air force investigated and admitted that the police officer was a credible witness and that they too were puzzled by what he saw.

Head for the **Very Large Array** (VLA), one of the world's top astronomical observatories. The VLA is located fifty miles west of Socorro on U.S. Highway 60. From U.S. 60, turn south on New Mexico 52, then west on the VLA access road, which is well marked. Signs will point you to the Visitor Center. Call 505-835-7000 for more information.

New York

HUDSON VALLEY/PINE BUSH

And you thought Manhattan was the place to be! New York's Hudson Valley area, north of New York City, is said to be by hundreds of newspaper and investigative reports by all the major UFO groups a consistent and anomalous area for craftlike objects and strange lights. No one is sure exactly what is flying around in the skies, only that things are. Though there's never a guarantee that you will see something or that what you will see will be a UFO, this is one of your best sighting opportunities on the East Coast.

The Story:

The valley was first hit by a wave of sightings of unidentified boomerang-shaped objects in 1982, with a peak of sightings in 1984. Sightings were reported in Brewster, Yorktown Heights, and over several reservoirs. Security guards at a nearby nuclear power plant allegedly spotted a boomerang-shaped UFO hovering between the tower and one of the reactor's dome's in July of 1984—it hovered for more than ten minutes and then bolted.

Pine Bush, New York, farther north on Hudson Valley in Orange

County, has become the best skywatching area in New York. The skies are clear and UFO activity has always been prevalent here. But as far as the locals are concerned, this is no Roswell. The locals are tolerant of skywatchers, but not thrilled by it.

Fabulous Pine Bush, New York— the Hottest of Hot Spots.

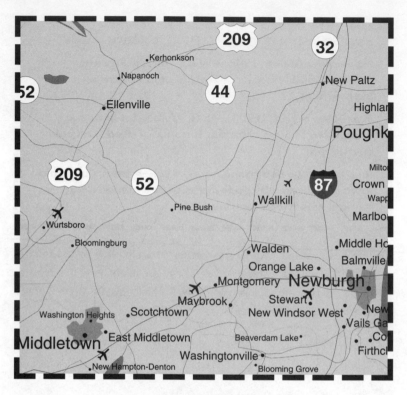

UFO Watching:

Local resident Beth Bley (proprietor of a local B&B) says good spots for viewing are out on Searsville Road and Drexel Road. There are no official observation areas, though you'll probably spot other skywatchers along these roads.

MANHATTAN

When ol' blue eyes sang about "the city that never sleeps," he was singing about the energy and excitement of the Big Apple. He probably never suspected that perhaps people weren't sleeping because they were afraid of being abducted.

The Story:

According to a report carried in several respected newspapers, including *The New York Times* and *The Wall Street Journal,* in September 1997 a car stalled near the South Street Seaport in Manhattan. The passengers in the car—a political figure and two government agents who have remained nameless—looked out the window of their car and allegedly saw a large oval object hovering over a nearby building. The object's lights supposedly started blinking, and a woman in a nightgown was allegedly pulled out of a twelfth-story window by three ugly little creatures and sucked inside the craft. The witnesses allegedly watched as the craft zipped over the Brooklyn Bridge and dove into the East River.

The woman was returned several hours later, and has worked extensively with Budd Hopkins, the founder and executive director of IF, the Intruders Foundation, an organization devoted to research and public education concerning the UFO abduction phenomenon. He has uncovered her many supposed abduction experiences, and has written *Intruders,* a famous book (in ufology circles) about alleged alien abductions. His was the first widely circulated and publicized book to make the claim that aliens are harvesting humans in order to breed them (now lots of people are making this claim).

UFO Watching:

There have been other reports of UFO activity near the **Manhattan side of the Brooklyn Bridge,** so any place that gives a good view of the bridge is a good spot for UFO hunting. But you just never know in New York. Witnesses standing on the street around **West 23rd Street and 7th Avenue** once reported seeing a green, oval object flying at an incredible rate of speed.

Or try skywatching from the Cathedral of the Skies—the **Empire**

State Building. Located at Fifth Avenue and 34th Street, 212-736-3100, Observatory: $6 adult, $3 senior & child under 12. Since its opening in 1931, the 1,453-foot skyscraper has attracted 120 million people to its observatories. Be sure to look up and not down!

North Carolina

• • • • • • • • • • • •

THE DEVIL'S TRAMPING GROUND/SILER CITY

Located about ten miles south of **Siler City** is an area of land with a thirty- to forty-foot circle in the woods where no vegetation will grow. Many believe this was once a well-used UFO landing spot. Debunkers agree that nothing will grow there—not because of aliens, but because so many people have been tramping around the area.

The Site:

To get to this crop circle, from Siler City, take U.S. 421 south. Turn right (southwest) on North Carolina 902. Drive approximately seven miles to Harper's Crossroads, turn right onto S.R. 1006. Almost immediately, take a left on S.R. 1100, also known as Devil's Tramping Ground Road. Drive about one-and-three-quarter miles. There will be a place on the left side of the road to pull off. There will be a sign that says "No Dumping Allowed." Park your car and walk the path about two hundred feet back into the woods.

MOUNT AIRY

Are there UFOs in Mayberry RFD? Is nothing sacred? But yes, it's possible that the real-life inspiration (and birthplace of the famous actor, Andy Griffith) for TV's popular **Mayberry RFD**—the town of Mount Airy—may be getting visits by unknown and unidentifiable guests flying in domed crafts. Today, Mount Airy still resembles a town spookily untouched by time. There's a drive-in movie and a drive-in restaurant.

The Story:

There have been regular UFO sightings in this famous little town since the early 1960s. The most recent case, as reported in the *Charlotte Observer*, took place in January 1997. A domed saucer was allegedly seen by several residents and sketched by two children. Also nearby is **Pilot Mountain** ("Mt. Pilot" on *The Andy Griffith Show*) which supplies its own steady stream of UFO reports. The Indians once believed this piece of mountain to be a sacred place. Some say extraterrestial biological entities (EBEs) are drawn to it too. The mountain is capped by two prominent pinnacles which offer spectacular opportunities for skywatching.

UFO Watching:
Pilot Mountain is located about twenty-five minutes north of Winston-Salem off Highway 52, and offers great skywatching. You can also camp, fish, climb, and hike here. It's located on Route 3, Box 21, Pinnacle, NC 27043.

North Dakota

. . . .

FARGO

Fargo is not exactly a hotbed of UFO activity—though residents have reported through the years that they have seen unusual, saucer-shaped craft near **Hector Airport.** Still, one of the classic cases in UFO history happened here.

The Story:

A lieutenant with the North Dakota Air National Guard reportedly had a twenty-seven minute "dogfight" (air force lingo for "air tag") with a UFO in the skies over Fargo. According to several accounts, including the air force's own report available to the public, the lieutenant told air force investigators that on the night of October 1, 1948, he had been on a cross-country flight with his squadron. Upon return to Hector Airport in Fargo, he elected to log some night flying time, so he remained airborne. He circled his F-51 over the lighted football stadium and around the city and was preparing to land when he spotted what appeared to be the tail-light of another plane that had passed him on the right. He reported the sighting to the tower, and insisted they didn't know about this plane.

The lieutenant decided to investigate the other aircraft and followed it. He described it as clear white, and completely round without fuzz at the

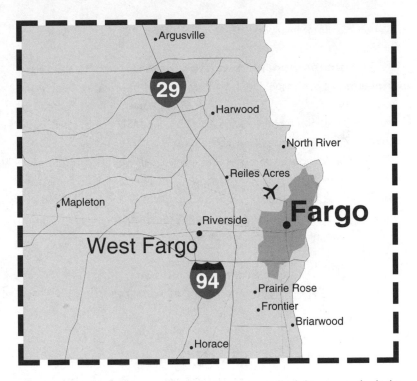

edges. It was blinking on and off. As he approached, however, the light suddenly became steady and pulled into a sharp left bank. The lieutenant gave chase, and says that at times during the chase, he pushed the F-51 to full power, sometimes reaching four hundred miles per hour. Then, he says, the object headed straight for his plane. But just when the object was about to hit his craft, it went into a steep climb and disappeared.

The lieutenant was so shaken by the encounter that he had difficulty handling his plane, although he was a veteran pilot and a flying instructor during World War II. Traffic controllers at the base also reported seeing a strange light traveling at intense speed near the airfield.

UFO Watching:

Hector Airport is located minutes from downtown Fargo at Nineteenth

Avenue North off Interstate 29. There are tons of signs. Just watch out for IFOs.

The planetarium at Moorhead State University's Science Center is just across the river from Fargo (1104 Seventh Avenue, Moorhead, MN 56563, 218-236-3982). The planetarium is located at Eleventh Street and Eighth Avenue South, on the MSU campus in Bridges Hall #167 in Moorhead, Minnesota.

The Center houses an observatory and hosts public astronomy lectures. It's open from 6 A.M. to 11 P.M. daily. The interpretive center is open from 1 to 5 P.M. on Sundays, from May 3 to October 25, with guided trail walks at 2 P.M. Entrance for public events, family astronomy nights, and to the site and interpretive center is free.

For More Information:
Fargo Travel Information, 800-235-7654.

Ohio
∙∙∙∙∙∙∙∙∙∙∙∙
CINCINNATI

In terms of recent UFO activity, this state ranks right up there with Arizona and North Carolina. It would be easier to list the Ohio towns that haven't reported a UFO sighting or some kind of related activity than those that have. And strangely enough, Cincinnati also shares a link with Roswell. In 1947, the *Cincinnati Post* and other news organizations reported that flying saucers were spotted over the city—the same week as the alleged Roswell crash took place. There was no official investigation at the time.

Fifty years later, there are still unknown things flying around in Cincinnati's skies. If you're interested in UFOs and a baseball fan, you're in luck.

The *Cincinnati Enquirer* reported alleged alien craft sightings over Cinergy Field, home of the Cincinnati Reds. Witnesses insist the starlike craft that was zipping around in the sky noiselessly above the field and the Ohio River was no blimp and no helicopter. Local UFO researcher Kenny Young also received a separate report of an alleged craft sighting on the same evening.

UFO Watching:

For premium skywatching and a good seventh inning stretch, head to **Cinergy Field.** For nonbaseball fans, head to the **Cincinnati Observatory,** located at 3489 Observatory Place, Cincinnati, OH 45208; 513-321-5186.

For More Information:

Visitors and Convention Bureau, 513-621-2142.

DAYTON

For years, **Wright-Patterson Air Force Base** located just outside of Dayton has been at the epicenter of Ohio UFO mysteries. There are dozens of articles and a lot of web speculation about this base's supposed alien-related activity.

The Story:

The base is the headquarters for air force research concerning new and foreign (alien, perhaps?) technologies. It was also home to **Project Bluebook,** the air force's official investigation of unidentified flying objects from 1947 to 1959. UFO conspiracy theorists and UFO skywatchers believe that **"Hangar 18"** (a.k.a. Hangar 13 and Building 18) is a secret, underground facility at the base. It is rumored to be where alien bodies were stored in a freezer after the 1947 alleged Roswell, New Mexico, crash of an alien spaceship. The military denies the existence of Hanger 18, but research groups, like the locally based TriState Advocates for Scientific Knowledge (TASK), say that military personnel have leaked information about Wright-Patterson's Roswell involvement. According to a 1997 article in the *Cincinnati Enquirer,* a TASK spokesperson said that Hangar 18 had been reported many times "by people in the military."

UFO Watching:

For skywatching head to the **Apollo Observatory at the Dayton Museum of Discovery,** open for public observing and/or astronomical programs every third Tuesday night from 7 to 9:00 P.M. (2600 DeWeese Parkway; 513-275-7431).

**Wright-Patterson
Air Force Base—
home of Project
Bluebook.**

During the Day:

Apparently, the military has a sense of humor. Wright-Patterson AFB recently opened the **Alien Alley Bowling Facility,** featuring a light show and glow-in-the-dark bowling (Friday and Saturday nights only). All active duty military, retired military, reservists, Department of Defense civilians, senior citizens, and their family members are eligible to use the facilities. If you fall into this category, call the bowling center for hours and number of lanes available. Call 937-257-7796 or go to Building 1221.

Oklahoma
....

CLINTON/SHERMAN AIR FORCE BASE

According to Cliff Capers, state director and newsletter editor for *Skywatch International*—a UFO investigative organization—this area around the Clinton-Sherman AFB may be Oklahoma's own "Area 51."

(See Nevada for the real Area 51.) Conveniently positioned for the traveling UFO hunter at the crossroads of Interstate 40 and U.S. Highway 183, there have been many recent sightings in this area. The alleged hot area is on I-40 between Clinton and Canute. A large white-glowing object was supposedly chasing cars here (about one- to two-hundred feet above the road).

The Site:

To get to the supposed flap area, head **west on I-40 from Clinton.** This stretch is about nineteen miles long.

The Clinton area is also home to **Foss State Park** (HC 60, Ross, OK 73647; 580-592-4433). According to Capers, this area, especially around the lake, is another potential hot spot. You can camp in the park too. See for yourself if there is more than just bass and perch gracing the lakes here. You can get there by heading eleven miles west of Clinton, then two miles north on Highway 44. (Or seven miles north of Foss on Highway 44.)

For More Information:
Clinton Chamber of Commerce, 580-323-2222.

ELK CITY

Oklahoma is known for many things—cowboys, horses, winds that come sweeping down the plains—and now, quite possibly, if you drive along I-40 near Elk City to mile marker 126 west of El Reno, UFOs. According to reports in several UFO newsletters, early in 1998, both green fireballs and quick-moving bright lights have been seen in the area. And according to Cliff Capers, Elk City is still a very active spot for UFO sightings.

The Story:
The UFO Roundup, an electronic newsletter edited by UFO researcher Joseph Trainor, reported that a local ufologist watched a fireball hit ground beyond the highway and throw up sparks. The next night the same witness reportedly saw a strange white light hovering above some trees near the Clinton/Sherman Air Force Base. The light supposedly shot off, hovered over I-40 for a few minutes, then vanished.

UFO Watching:
Your best bet for viewing is to head to **I-40 around mile marker 47,** where recent activity has been reported.

Oregon
· · · · · · · · · · · ·
ALBANY

The city of Albany is located on Interstate 5, between Eugene and Salem. It's a mere hour from Portland in western Oregon. According to several witnesses, something weird is going on here.

The Story:
Starting in late March and early April 1997, residents began reporting

that they were seeing unexplained lights. The lights were usually round and orange, and came as mysteriously as they went. Many residents believe they are UFOs. Albany has a previous UFO history of crafts and light anomalies—according to Greg Long, the most prominent researcher and writer of UFO and paranormal activity for the Pacific Northwest. And according to the local Albany newspaper, the *Oregon Herald,* in the 1970s this area was the scene of several mysterious and unexplainable cattle mutilations.

The Sites:

For skywatching, head just outside of town, east on **U.S. Highway 20.** There are several open fields, no lights, and lots of wide-open skies.

You can also travel to the **Foster Reservoir** in nearby Sweet Home, about forty miles from Albany. Go east on U.S. 20 to Interstate 5 south, then to State Route 34 heading east, then back to U.S. 20 for eight miles. You will see loads of signs for the reservoir; it's a major outdoors recreational area for Oregonians.

Foster Reservoir is partially inside and partially outside of Sweet Home, Oregon, just north of Highway 20. **Sweet Home** is on the Santiam River in the foothills of the Cascades. It stretches along the highway for several miles. The reservoir forms behind Green Peter Dam, which is located up a paved road that will take you up in elevation to premium skywatching territory in Quartzville farther north. Long also received a dramatic alleged alien craft sighting from campers in Quartzville—so who knows . . . and if you strike out seeing anything in the sky, look into the forest, for this part of Oregon is said to be prime Big Foot country (as if camping wasn't challenging enough)!

For More Information

Sweet Home Ranger District, 3225 Highway 20, Sweet Home, OR 97386, 541-367-5168. Greg Long's very comprehensive web site is found at www.nwmyst.com.

THE OREGON VORTEX

?

Grants Pass is truly a mysterious area in the southern part of Oregon, and is worth a visit. This is where a perplexing vortex that the Indians called the "forbidden ground" is located. The famous Rouge River brings many visitors to Grants Pass, but for more than sixty years scientists, ufologists, and the plain old curious have been flocking here to solve the riddle of the vortex located within the wooded terrain near **Gold Hill.**

> *"IN THE FIRM BELIEF THAT THE AMERICAN PUBLIC DESERVES A BETTER EXPLANATION THAN THAT THUS FAR GIVEN BY THE AIR FORCE, I STRONGLY RECOMMEND THAT THERE BE A COMMITTEE INVESTIGATION [OF THE UFO PHENOMENON]."*
>
> **Congressman [later President] Gerald Ford, 1966**

Located sixty-three miles south of Roseburg at the junction of Interstate 5 and U.S. 199, the Vortex is an area on a hillside that measures about three-quarters of an acre. A beat-up old shack on the site (once an office of a mining company there) has been dubbed the "house of mystery" because of the strange phenomena that occur within it. People seem to change size and shape inside the shack, and lean at odd angles despite standing on flat ground. Many in the UFO world believe that vortices are either caused by aliens or are an attraction for them.

The Site:

The House of Mystery at the Oregon Vortex is located at 4303 Sardine Creek Road, Gold Hill, Oregon 97525. For brochures and information call 541-855-1543. (Hours: June-August, 8:30 A.M. to 6:00 P.M.; March-May, September, and October, 9:30 A.M. to 4:30 P.M.; admission for 12 and older $7.00; ages 5 to 11, $5.00; younger than 5 get in for free.)

For More Information:
Grants Pass Visitors and Convention Bureau, 541-476-5510.

Pennsylvania

••••••••••••

KECKSBURG

The small, rural town of Kecksburg is located in southwestern Pennsylvania, about forty miles southeast of Pittsburgh. And though it's admittedly less glamorous and alien-oriented than Roswell, it's nonetheless a significant crash site in the annals of UFO history.

The Story:

According to multiple local newspaper accounts, on December 9, 1965 a fiery object tore across the sky, with thousands of witnesses from Michigan to New York. Reports of debris from the object were made in many states. Most witnesses thought they were seeing a plane going down in flames. But as it came in for its crash in Kecksburg's woods, witnesses reportedly said it wasn't a plane. They say they saw a blue column of smoke arise and then dissipate. Local volunteer fire companies combed the woods, searching for the wreck. The state police also arrived, to coordinate the search as well as keep order (radio and TV news reports of the mysterious object had drawn crowds of curious onlookers to the site).

A state police fire marshal, accompanied by an unidentified man carrying a Geiger counter supposedly descended into the woods. Onlookers and the media were told that nothing had crashed. Yet shortly thereafter, the woods were sealed off by state police and most curiously, the town was soon swarming with military vehicles.

Later that night witnesses reported seeing a military flatbed truck come out of the woods. Lashed on top of it was a large, tarp-shrouded object. Its shape has been described as resembling an enormous acorn, mushroom, or bullet. Then came the military's explanation—a meteorite had fallen.

But other eyewitnesses have emerged through the years. One has said that at the time of the crash, he was called from nearby Latrobe to serve on a search team. He emphatically insists that the object was no known type of aircraft or rocket. It was a solid piece of some unknown metal that was shaped like an acorn. There were no doors or windows. It gave off no smoke or vapors.

Stan Gordon, of the Pennsylvania Association for the Study of the Unexplained (PASU), is an avid Kecksburg researcher and has made a fascinating documentary of the case called *Kecksburg—The Untold Story*. He believes that evidence shows that the military was covering something up. The crash remains unsolved. Gordon has documented and investigated many reports of UFOs in Western Pennsylvania.

To read more about the alleged alien crash site and for other sightings in Western Pennsylvania, check out Stan Gordon's web site: www.westol.com/~paufo.

The Sites:
In Kecksburg, visit **the firehouse** in the center of town to see a replica of the UFO used for a filming of *Unsolved Mysteries*. The crash site is located on private property, but is close to the firehouse.

UFO Watching:
Forbes State Forest is a good spot for skywatching in this area of Pennsylvania. For more information contact: Forbes State Forest, PO Box 519, Laughlintown, PA 15655; 724-238-9533.

During the Day:
If you do have a sighting and need to kick a few back and calm down, visit the nearby **Latrobe Brewing Company,** the makers of Rolling Rock beer. There is a visitor's center, a gift shop, and cheap beer. It's located at 119 Jefferson Street, Latrobe, PA 15650; 724-539-3394.

Rhode Island
••••••••••••
PROVIDENCE

America's first shopping mall—"The Arcade"—was built here in 1828. Perhaps that explains the mysterious alleged appearance of "black helicopters" here. Aliens are mall rats at heart.

The Story:
Black helicopters are mysterious military craft thought to be associated with UFO sightings and/or Men in Black (see page 44). They are also reportedly seen in areas where cattle mutilations take place (though that is not the case here). Rhode Island is not known for sightings (probably

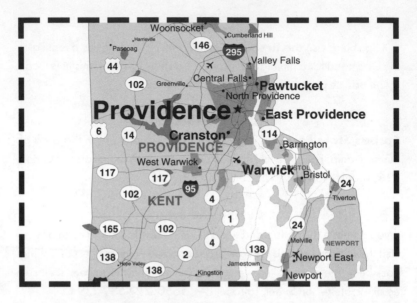

because of its tiny size), but several black helicopter sightings have been reported, and if you see one, chances are you will be near Providence, the state's capital.

Several independent witnesses have also reported seeing triangular-shaped UFOs on Route 10 in the Olney section of Providence. The objects allegedly had three very bright lights and hovered and rotated for several minutes, then rose vertically and flew away very quickly.

UFO Watching:

If you don't feel like camping out in your car on Highway 10, try sky-watching in **Roger Williams Memorial Park** (282 North Main Street; 401-521-7266). It's located right in downtown Providence, one block from the State House. From Interstate 95 north or south, take the downtown exit; turn left at the first light onto Francis Street; turn right at the next light across from the State House; turn right at the next light onto Smith Street; turn right at the next light onto Canal Street. You will see the entrance to the parking lot on your left.

During the Day:
The Cormack Planetarium is located within the **Natural History Museum** in Providence. The Museum is open daily from 10 A.M. to 5 P.M. but the planetarium is only open on weekends and holidays. Call 401-785-9457 for more information. To get there take I-95 south to Exit 17 (Elmwood Ave.) Turn left at the light. The park entrance is the second left.

For More Information:
Providence Convention and Visitors Bureau,
401-274-1636 or 800-233-1636.

South Carolina
....

MYRTLE BEACH

Myrtle Beach has its share of reported UFO sightings each year, but none seem to top the historical January 29, 1953 close encounter that allegedly took place there.

The Story:
One famous account (as told in the *Charlotte Observer*) was of a Horry County resident who apparently heard his chickens and ducks squawking in an irregular fashion. He grabbed his twenty-two caliber pistol and went to investigate.

He supposedly spotted a gray saucer hovering over a row of pine trees on his property, and fired five shots. Each shot ricocheted off the saucer's metallic surface, he reported, and the saucer flew away. This case generated a media blitz at the time, and was well documented by UFO investigators. The navy claimed the resident had encountered a blimp.

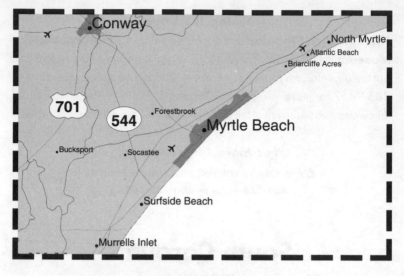

UFO Watching:

This area of South Carolina is said to be a good UFO sighting area because of its large coasts (apparently aliens like beaches too). Actually, some believers theorize that UFOs may need water for their cooling systems. **Litchfield Beach** (a glamorous resort area located about twenty miles south of Myrtle Beach) is another area where sightings have occurred. To get to Litchfield Beach, head west on Highway 707—then pick up Highway 17 heading southwest.

South Dakota

···········

ELLSWORTH

Ellsworth Air Force Base sits just seven miles from Rapid City, South Dakota—the Black Hills area of the Badlands. Great attractions, including Mt. Rushmore National Memorial, are located near here. And Ellsworth AFB, as well as the Badlands area in general, is probably South Dakota's hottest UFO spot.

The Story:

The base's most bizarre case was the alleged November 1977 incident in which security guards observed a bright light shining vertically up from the rear of a fence in front of a small hill. When one of the guards approached the hill, he reportedly saw two entities dressed in green metallic uniforms and helmets with visors.

The intruders apparently refused to stop and started to walk toward the fence. One allegedly aimed an object that emitted a flash of light at the guard, hit his rifle, disintegrated it, and burned the officer's hands. He took cover and requested help. Another guard fired at the entities, and they eventually headed back over the hill. One of the guards followed, and allegedly witnessed them entering a saucer-shaped craft glowing with green light. The UFO then supposedly quickly rose vertically and whooshed out of sight.

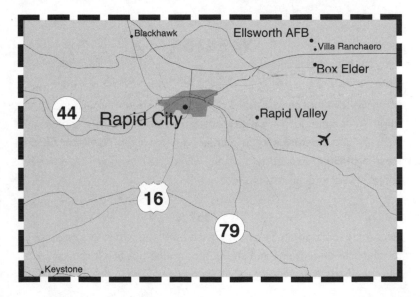

UFO Watching:

For excellent viewing head to the **Badlands National Park** (fifty-one miles east of Rapid City on Interstate 90). You'll find some very cool rock formations and good plateaus for checking out the sky.

You might also try the **Mt. Rushmore National Memorial** (twenty-five miles southwest of Rapid City Highway 16A; 605-574-2515). You may not see aliens, but you will see some awfully big heads.

During the Day:

Visit the **South Dakota Air and Space Museum** located right on **Ellsworth AFB** (from Rapid City take I-90 east to Exit 66 and follow the signs to the base on Scott Drive; 605-385-5188). To make arrangements for a group tour (no individual tours), call 605-385-5056. The base hosts a big open house air show in August; call 605-385-4414 for information.

For More Information:

Rapid City Convention and Visitors Bureau, 1-800-487-3223.

YANKTON

Many believe that certain tribes of Native Americans have had secret, ongoing communications with extraterrestrials for hundreds of years. According to Standing Elk, the spiritual advisor of the **Yankton Sioux Reservation** in southeastern South Dakota, the time may have come for contact to occur at his reservation.

The Story:

According to Standing Elk, a ufologist himself, he was told by a Spirit to reach out to other races and share information about extraterrestrials. Thus, the **Star Knowledge Conference** was born, for this very purpose. At each conference, Native Americans share with each other and the general public teachings about the Star Nations' (what the Native Americans call extraterrestrials) communications and interaction with Indian tribes. For further information about the annual Star Knowledge Conference which is held in a different city each year, contact: Standing Elk/Loren Zephier, c/o Yankton Sioux Reservation, Post Office Box 120, Marty, SD 57361, 605-384-5152.

The Site:

To visit the reservation, call 1-800-888-1460 for a free vacation packet, or write the Chamber of Commerce, P.O. Box 588W, Yankton, SD 57078.

Tennessee

OAK RIDGE

Cloaked in secrecy during the World War II years, Oak Ridge (or the "Atomic City") was the site of the **Manhattan Project,** the code name for the atom bomb project. This pretty and still mysterious place about twenty miles from Knoxville lies between Great Smoky Mountains on the southeast and the Cumberland Mountains on the northwest. The views are incredible here—and so is this National Laboratory's long history of UFO phenomenon. (Note: The researchers for the Manhattan Project are not to be referred to as "The Oak Ridge Boys.")

The Story:

Several of Oak Ridge's most notable events occurred in the early 1950s. The Air Force's Project Bluebook documents tell the chilling tale. An Atomic Energy Security Patrol Trooper reportedly saw a pear-shaped craft that

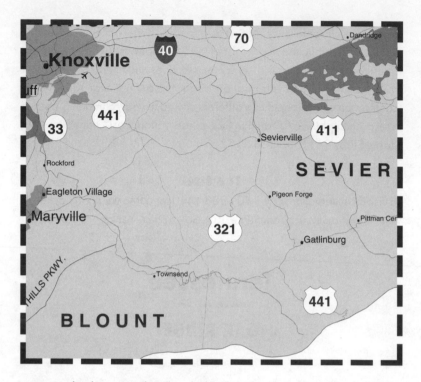

appeared to have a tail trailing behind it. The object apparently tried to clear a fence around a secured area, and when the trooper approached, the object became smaller, gained altitude, and flew away. The object ostensibly reappeared but was never intercepted. There has never been a satisfactory answer as to what was flying in the skies around this sensitive area.

The Site:

Today, **Oak Ridge National Laboratory** (a large complex—the main access road is the Oak Ridge Turnpike) is a science and technology laboratory that still conducts activities related to national security. It is now possible to visit the inside of the laboratory by arrangement. Call 423-574-4160.

Tours:
The American Museum of Science and Energy located near the main campus hosts a public tour of two Oak Ridge facilities. The museum is located at 300 South Tulane Avenue, Oak Ridge, TN 37830; 423-576-3200. It is open daily from 9:00 A.M. to 5:00 P.M. Admission is free. With advance notice, ORNL also provides guided group tours of laboratory facilities. For information, please contact the Office of Public Affairs, P.O. Box 2008, Oak Ridge, TN 37831-6266; 423-574-4160. Public tours beginning at the **American Museum of Science and Energy** in Oak Ridge, Tennessee, are available from March through October.

Visitors may take a free self-guided driving tour. The two tour stops—the **New Bethel Church and the Graphite Reactor**—are open seven days a week, from 9 A.M. to 5 P.M., including holidays.

For More Information:
Oak Ridge Visitor's Information, 1-800-887-3429.

Texas
....
HOUSTON

Houston is a spaced-out city. Area attractions include Space Center Houston and professional sport teams such as the Houston Astros and Houston Rockets—you get the idea—and if you don't, there's something alien about you.

But the spaciest thing to allegedly take place in the Houston area was the famous **Cash-Lundrum UFO case.**

The Story:
According to dozens of sources, including the book *The Cash-Landrum Inci-*

dent by John Schuessler, on December 29, 1980, Betty Cash and Vickie Landrum allegedly encountered a diamond-shaped UFO on a road near the town of Huffman. They reported that the UFO emitted unbearable heat, and they were injured with radiation-type exposure. As the UFO departed, several helicopters reportedly swarmed into the area and chased it.

The strange case was documented by an aerospace manager and was later investigated by the USAF Inspector's General Office, who could account for neither the craft nor for the helicopters chasing it.

The Sites:
Drive along **Highway FM 1485** until you are near Huffman—this is the area where the sighting allegedly took place. This road is usually used only by people who live in the area, because it is so isolated. Although it's close to Houston, the area is sparsely populated and is covered by oak and pine trees, and dotted with swamps and lakes. Bring a flashlight—you may need it.

UFO Watching:
For up-to-the-minute sighting news in Houston call **HUFON** at 281-597-2834. This UFO investigative group's meetings are open to the general public and are held at 7:00 P.M. on the second Saturday of each month at the Holiday Inn at 7787 Katy Freeway. Take Interstate 10, Antoine exit, just outside the Loop 610, south side.

During the Day:
Visit the hometown of America's astronauts! **Space Center Houston** (1601 NASA Road One; 281-244-2105) is ground zero for a visit to the NASA/Johnson Space Center. This visitor's center and museum explores the past, present, and future of manned space flight through exhibits of retired spacecraft, space suits, and moon rock; IMAX films; computer-simulated opportunities to land a space shuttle or launch a satellite; and guided tours through astronaut training facilities at Johnson Space Center.

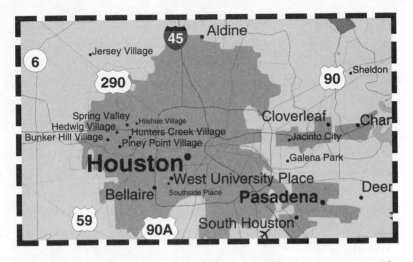

It is located twenty-five miles south of downtown Houston via Interstate 45.

The Houston Museum of Natural Science (1 Hermann Circle Drive; 713-639-4600) is home to the Burker Baker Planetarium and Worthman IMAX Theater.

The Lone Star Flight Museum is more than eighty thousand square feet and exhibits a variety of displays including more than thirty-five vintage aircraft. The Lone Star Flight Museum is also custodian to the Eighth Air Force 303rd Bomb Group. It offers tours and operates from 10 A.M. to 5 P.M. daily. The museum is located at Galveston's Scholes Field, next to Moody Gardens. For admission costs and times, call 888-FLIGHT-8.

If you're not totally worn out you might also want to visit **The Science Place** (1318 Second Avenue, Fair Park; 214-428-5555). It offers a planetarium and IMAX Dome Theater.

MARFA

Nine miles east of the Texas city of Marfa, far out into the west Texas desert at the base of the Chianti Mountains lies another **mystery of lights.**

The Story:

According to the Marfa Chamber of Commerce, the Ghost Lights of Marfa are small orbs that float, glow, change shape and color, and have no known source. They have made this town a mecca for those seeking the strange and the unexplainable. Thousands of tourists flock here each year to witness the ghostly lights with their own eyes. Chances are you will see these active orbs—you just can't get too close. The lights will disappear if you do.

The lights were first reported more than a century ago by the first settlers in the area. The Apache Indians before them believed the mysterious lights were stars dropping to Earth. Of course there's always the contingent that says the lights are caused by extraterrestrial sources. Who knows?

The Site:

There is an official **Marfa Lights Viewing Site.** It's on Highway 90, nine miles east of Marfa. There's a big sign; you can't miss it. If you see something unusual, send a written account of it to: Mystery Lights, P.O. Box 195, Alpine, TX 79831. Binoculars are helpful but not necessary. Marfa also hosts a **Light Festival** in September. For tickets and information, contact the Marfa Chamber of Commerce at 800-650-9696.

Utah

CACHE COUNTY

Crop circles, which are thought to be the result of alien craft, are most prevalent in the United Kingdom—and in Utah.

The Story:

In 1996, according to accounts detailed in the *Salt Lake City Tribune* and the *Star Beacon,* circles began appearing in Cache County, in the Smithfield and Providence areas about eighty-five miles north of Salt Lake City. Crop circle researchers from Canada were stunned to discover there had been at least five crop formations since July 1997 in the general area.

The most dramatic circles allegedly appeared on a barley field that lies on Highway 91 just outside the town of Smithfield. Two-and-a-half-foot stalks of barley were supposedly found, perfectly laid down with no broken kernels and no disturbed rocks. Witnesses also reported that a compass would spin wildly if you held it inside the circle. Other witnesses said if you sat inside the circle you could hear a high-pitched sound.

The Site:

For a time the farm was swamped with visitors, and the family had to put up no trespassing signs because their barley was getting trampled. Moreover, crop circles grow out rather quickly, so unless there's been a recent incident, there won't be much to see. But keep your eyes and ears peeled

Map of Cache County showing: Smithfield, Logan, Hyde Park, North Logan, River Heights, Providence, Millville, Nibley, Newton, Hyrum, and CACHE.

as you pass through the town of **Smithfield,** and you may find what you're looking for.

GREEN RIVER

Could the new Area 51 be located near the snoozing town of Green River? Ever since the highly debated and controversial article in *Popular Mechanics* (June 1997), people are wondering. And according to lots of web reports, some say the skywatching is now as good as the fishing there—which is to say, damn good.

The Story:

Conspiracy theorists believe that due to all of the publicity surrounding Nevada's Area 51, the military had to find a new location for its secret technology development and covert alien research. That location, many believe, is a remote army facility in eastern Utah.

The facility's official name is the **Utah Launch Complex.** The 3,650-acre complex sits in the hills north of Moab, and was established in 1961 to test missiles. It was closed in the early seventies. But within the last year, residents of Green River have reported increased activity and a lot of strange things flying around in their skies. The roads have also recently been repaired and security has been stepped up.

UFO Watching:

From Green River, take Interstate 70 to Exit 162 and head south. You will soon come to a "T" intersection and turn left. This puts you on the main road of Green River Launch Complex.

For More Information:
Utah Travel Info, 800-UTAH-FUN.

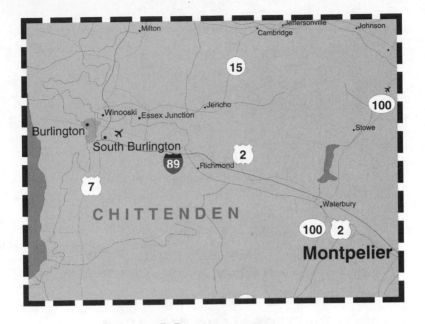

Vermont

••••••••••••

LAKE CHAMPLAIN

Lake Champlain is the largest freshwater lake in the United States out-side the Great Lakes. It's also ostensibly the home to a **monster,** which some believe is an alien left from a long-ago UFO crash—its name is **"Champ."**

The Story:

As dozens of newspaper and magazine accounts tell it, including *Time* magazine, Champ is a serpentlike creature who was first reportedly seen in the late 1800s and allegedly continues to appear to this day. According to a *Strangemag* article by Mark Chorvinsky, the largest mass sighting occurred in 1984, when tourists on a sightseeing boat near Appletree Point saw the monster rise up. It's been called the American Loch Ness Monster and has been sighted several hundred times. Witnesses say it's about twenty-five or thirty feet in length, has a humped back, and white spots inside its mouth. Some say he looks like a dinosaur. Happy swimming!

The Site:
To get to Lake Champlain, head for Burlington—the lake is right on the edge of the city.

For More Information:
Lake Champlain Regional Chamber of Commerce, 802-863-3489.
Vermont Department of Travel and Tourism, 800-VERMONT.

WESTFORD AND RICHFORD

Vermont isn't only for cow and ice cream lovers anymore—it's for UFO lovers as well.

The Story:
According to Davy Russell, writing in *X-Project Paranormal Magazine,* the majority of reported UFO sightings and encounters takes place around the **northwest part of the state** (around the towns of Westford and Richford), and along Route 7 going north along the Canadian border. The **Connecticut River,** which borders Vermont and New Hampshire, has also had its share of alleged UFO phenomena.

Although these areas appear to be the most active, UFOs have been reported in every county, and probably every town in Vermont. Descriptions have ranged from craft-shaped saucers, cigars, cylinders, boomerangs, triangles, and bathtubs. A Bennington sighting once described a "flying silo."

In addition, for the past fifty years, red, glowing balls of light have been reported in the East Fairfield and Bakersfield area (also called the "Lost Nation"). Farmers have allegedly seen these small lights numerous times for many years. So far, no one has figured out what they are.

UFO Watching:

For an amazing viewing location, from Bakersfield, turn left opposite the cemetery onto unmarked Route 36. Three miles west is East Fairfield. Stay on Route 36 through East Fairfield, and in five miles you'll enter **Fairfield.** When you crest a hill six miles west of Fairfield, you will see an incredible view of the upper **Champlain Valley,** with St. Albans in the foreground, Lake Champlain in the middle distance, and New York's Adirondacks as a backdrop.

Virginia
....

ARLINGTON

The Pentagon, headquarters of the Department of Defense, is one of the world's largest office buildings. It's virtually its own city. And it was also the home of Project Bluebook, the official investigation of the UFO phenomena by the air force. It began in 1948 and ended in 1969.

The Story:

In response to public pressure for answers as to what the heck is flying around the nation's skies, the air force began **Project Bluebook** (also known as Project Grudge because many felt the government's heart was

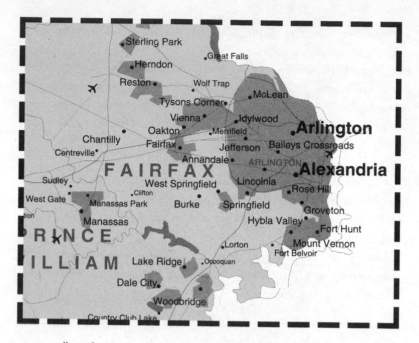

never really in the investigation). By the time it ceased operations twenty-one years later, more than twelve thousand UFO reports had been examined under the project. Seven hundred and one of those cases remain unsolved—but it was never established whether or not aliens were involved.

Critics say Project Bluebook and then later the Condon Committee, under which it was reorganized, was the military's debunking effort. Today, the Pentagon's official stand on UFOs is that the government doesn't believe in them. All documentation regarding Project Bluebook was permanently transferred to the Military Reference Branch, National Archives and Records Administration, Eighth and Pennsylvania Avenue, Washington, D.C. 20408, and is available for public review.

The Site:

The Pentagon is in Arlington, Virginia, immediately west of the Potomac River. A visitor parking lot is available in the Hayes Street commercial parking lot, 700 Army-Navy Drive, Pentagon City. The lot is directly across the street from Macy's department store (call for extra twenty-percent-off days). Walk-in tours and group tours (for ten or more arranged in advance) are available Monday through Friday and are free. Requests for group tours can be sent via the Internet (tourschd@osd.pentagon.mil); faxed (703) 614-1642; or can be mailed to: Director, Pentagon Tours, Room 1E776, 1400 Defense Pentagon, Washington, D.C. 20301-1400. Call 703-695-1776 for more information.

VIRGINIA BEACH

Virginia Beach has a grand history of UFO activity. In 1994, the Virginian-Pilot reported an alleged mass sighting of a **fireball.** According to a local skywatcher, an earlier fireball appeared in the 1970s and hundreds of people on the boardwalk claim to have witnessed strange craft flying out over the ocean. They were allegedly amber-colored, and darted about quickly, not moving like airplanes at all. And according to Laura Miller, a MUFON field investigator, it looks like Virginia Beach may be heating up again. One recent sighting involved a round metallic disc that allegedly flew in from over the ocean—it was glowing, silent, and moving very fast.

UFO Watching:

Most of this area's UFO activity seems to originate from the ocean, so head to **the beach** and the three-mile stretch of boardwalk for the best skywatching.

For More Information:
City of Virginia Beach Convention and Visitor Center,
800-VA-BEACH or 757-437-4888.

Washington

MOUNT RAINIER

Did you ever wonder who coined the term *flying saucer?* It was made up by Kenneth Arnold, a pilot and businessman who on June 24, 1947 witnessed the **first official American UFO sighting.**

The Story:

According to hundreds of newspaper and accounts told in UFO books, including *The Encyclopedia of UFOs* edited by Ronald D. Story, Kenneth Arnold was flying to Yakima, Washington, on a beautiful and clear day. The flight was going smoothly until he allegedly saw some bright flashes of light from the corner of his eye. When he turned his head, he reportedly saw nine bright objects hovering about ninety-five hundred feet above the ground. The objects were heading toward Mt. Rainier at about seventeen hundred miles an hour. At first, Arnold thought they were airplanes. But as he kept watching them—flying in and out of Mt. Rainer's peaks, he noticed there were no wings on the boomerang-shaped objects.

Eventually the news media heard about it, and when Arnold was interviewed by a reporter and asked to describe what he saw, he compared their motion to skimming saucers. The reporter then put the words *flying saucer* in his article about Arnold.

Mount Rainier—where flying saucers were born.

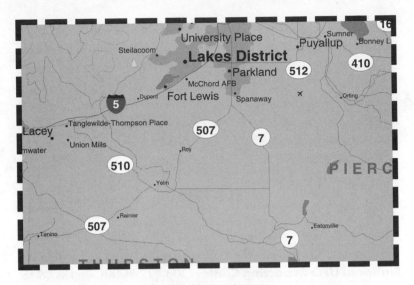

UFO Watching:

Mount Rainier National Park (Tahoma Woods, Star Route, Ashford, WA 98304-9751; 360-569-2211) is located in west-central Washington, approximately one to two hours driving time from Seattle, Tacoma, and Yakima, Washington, and Portland, Oregon. Though there haven't been any UFO reports as dramatic as Arnold's since then, there have been tales of UFOs. Your best bet for viewing is to get as high up as you can. **Sunrise Point** at sixty four hundred feet is the highest point in the park reached by road. The months of July and September are when the higher trails are

UFO WATCHING ON MT. ST. HELENS

Many believe that volcanoes are an attraction of sorts for extraterrestrial visitors, and now you can find out for yourself. To see UFOs on Mount St. Helens, take **Spirit Lake Highway to the Johnston Ridge Observatory,** at milepost 53.8. This is the end of the road for visitors, but for skywatchers it's just the beginning. Plus there's an awesome view of the crater. This is a Forest Service site, so fees are required.

usually free of snow. The National UFO Reporting Center had a 1998 report of a very bright UFO hovering near the mountain on the north side.

Mount Rainier is accessible from several directions via Interstate 5, U.S. Highway 12, and State Routes 7, 706, 123, 410, and 165. Lodging is available within the park. For information and reservations, call 360-569-2275 or write to Mount Rainier Guest Services, Incorporated, P.O. Box 108, Ashford, WA 98304. Call 800-365-CAMP to make campground reservations.

SEATTLE

The largest UFO hotline in the United States is based in Seattle—the **National UFO Reporting Center** (206-722-3000). And its hometown keeps investigators busy. Seattle has had quite a few mass sightings.

The Story:

There doesn't seem to be any one spot that UFOs are attracted to around this city. According to reports received by the center, UFOs have appeared near highways and over the Woodland Park Zoo. But one unbeatable place for skywatching is this city's most famous attraction— the Seattle Space Needle—the top of which is shaped like a flying saucer. Maybe it's as close as UFOs get to family here on Earth.

The Site:

The Space Needle (located in Seattle center on Mercer Avenue, a large campuslike area encompassing a great many buildings) is open 365 days a year (Observation Deck open from 8:00 A.M. to midnight; Needle Lounge open daily from 12:00 P.M. To 11:00 P.M.). Admission is as follows: $9.00 for adults, $8.00 for seniors, $4.00 for children 5 to 12, and free for children 4 and under.

From Interstate 5 north or south, take Mercer Street/Seattle Center

Exit 167, following the signs leading to Seattle Center. It takes just forty-three seconds in a glass elevator from ground level to 520 feet above Seattle. You won't take off at warp speed but its restaurant on top does revolve (slowly enough to enjoy your Lunar Orbiter Dessert). And it's a great place to catch one of the many UFOs that have reportedly been flying over and around Seattle for years. It also offers a coffee shop and gift shop.

Washington, D.C.

·············

?

"Take me to your leader," say the aliens in the movies, emerging from the saucer, rayguns in hand. But when a wave of unexplained aerial activity hit the nation's capital in the early 1950s, many people were wondering if perhaps the aliens hadn't found our leaders already.

The Story:
According to articles in just about every national newspaper, including the *New York Times,* and the air force's own press releases, panic very nearly erupted after air traffic controllers from Andrews Air Force Base and Washington National Airport tracked on radar several fast-moving objects, or "unknowns," in flight over the city. Pilots coming in and out of the airport as well as witnesses on the ground also reportedly saw the objects, which were characterized as bright lights. In July 1952, there were as many as a dozen unknowns reported on radar screens.

The media went wild, printing headlines that Washington was being invaded by foreign or alien powers. The largest peacetime press conference in U.S. history was called to explain to reporters that these "radar traces" were caused by thermal inversions, although the weather conditions on the nights of the sightings did not support that explanation. Subsequent, inexplicable sightings have occurred at the airport and in the skies over Washington D.C. Most recently, in 1997, witnesses have reported seeing a dark, crescent-shaped object flying over the city at a high rate of speed.

UFO Watching:

For skywatching, head to the **South Memorial Bridge.** There is a pedestrian walkway here and the paths for Gravelly Point Park runs alongside the George Washington Memorial Parkway. This park is located both in the District and in Arlington, Virginia. If you pick it up near the bridge on the D.C. side and head south, you will eventually come to an area where you will have a clear view of a plane runway for National Airport. You'll know when you're there because planes fly right over your head. Let's just hope there're no leaky fuel tanks!

During the Day:

Be sure to visit **Dream Wizards,** home of **Strange Bookshop** (of *Strange Magazine* fame), when in the Washington, D.C. area. Dream Wizards features UFO and other paranormal topics. It's at 104G Halpine Road, Rockville, Maryland 20852 (near 1749 Rockville Pike). Call 301-881-3530 for directions.

Don't miss **The Smithsonian Institution's National Air and Space Museum** (on the National Mall at Seventh and Independence Avenue, S.W., Washington, D.C., just west of the Capitol Building). It houses the largest collection of historic air- and spacecraft in the world. The museum has hundreds of artifacts on display, including the original Wright 1903 Flyer and the Apollo 11 command module. The museum also houses the **Samuel P. Langley IMAX Theater** and the **Albert Einstein Planetarium.** The museum is open every day except December 25, from 10:00 A.M. to 5:30 P.M. General admission is free. For more information on tours, programs, science demonstrations, or to make reservations, call the Tours and Reservations Office at 202-357-1400. General Smithsonian information: 202-357-2700.

West Virginia

....

POINT PLEASANT

?

Folks will tell you "we're visiting Point Pleasant for its rich history—it was the scene of the American Revolution's first battle." But don't believe them. They're probably really here to catch a glimpse of **the Mothman.**

The Story:

Point Pleasant is located on the Ohio River in Mason County and on the far western side of the state. There is no shortage of information and stories circulating in print and on the web about its most famous resident, the alleged Mothman. One of the best, most balanced web accounts is told by Troy Taylor at **www.prairieghosts.com.** According to Taylor and several other sources, the monster was allegedly first spotted in an abandoned military facility. This area, right outside of Point Pleasant was used to manufacture explosives during World War II and is thus known as the "TNT" area.

On November 15, 1966 two young couples were ostensibly cruising the TNT area "looking (wink, wink) for friends." (The area was, and still is, a great place for hanging out, making out, and partying in general.) There they reportedly saw the Mothman, a six-foot-tall creature with red glowing eyes and a wingspread of ten feet, by the north power plant—and it started chasing them. They drove as fast as they could back to town, but when they looked back they found it was still chasing them. (The Mothman has been reported to travel at one hundred miles per hour.) They also state that

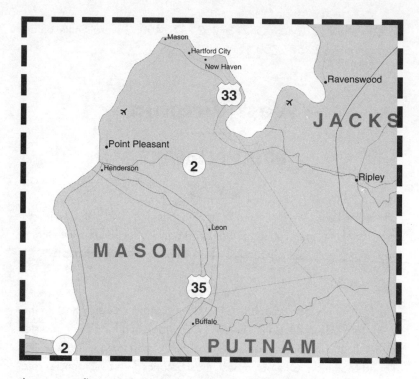

they saw it fly straight up into the sky without flapping its wings. They reported the incident to the local police. On November 16, an editor of the *Athens Messenger* christened the creature "Mothman" and the name stuck.

The Mothman was reportedly seen more than a hundred times over the next year. Usually because people left their porch lights on. Kidding.

The Site:

Your best shot of seeing the Mothman is at **the TNT area** and along **Highway 62** in the dark and creepy dead of night. Point Pleasant lies one mile north of junction U.S. 35 and West Virginia 2 or at the intersection of West Virginia Routes 62 and 2 in Mason County. There is a park at the intersection of Routes 62 and 2 just west of this intersection at One Main Street where camping is permitted.

Wisconsin

ELMWOOD

Elmwood is a small town with a big and celebrated UFO history—so big in fact that the town holds a **UFO festival** the last full weekend in July.

The Story:

According to the town's own literature and many newspaper accounts, it all started on March 2, 1975 when a local resident was allegedly chased by a starlike object in her car. At first she thought it was a satellite, as did other witnesses. But when it supposedly followed her home and landed on the hood of her car, she began to think extraterrestrially. The object allegedly flew into the air above some trees and was seen by several people.

In another UFO incident, a local police officer and several others apparently saw and almost encountered a huge flaming ball. It allegedly

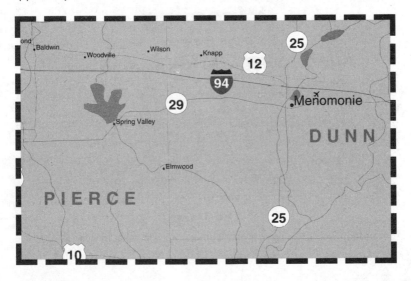

hit the officer's squad car and burned out all of its plugs and points. Many other sightings have followed over the years—seeing a UFO in and around this town of one thousand became quite commonplace.

The town's **"UFO Days Celebration"** began in 1978, and has become a yearly celebration. The festival's main highlight is a parade on Sunday. In between there's a lot of homespun and fun stuff to do, like polka dancin' and pancake eatin'. Call 715-639-4132.

The Site:

Elmwood is located in the wooded hills of eastern Pierce County, ninety-three miles northwest of North Bend. It's close to many natural recreation areas and state parks. Lodging during the festival is available in town at Elmwood Inn. Call 715-639-3872.

For More Information:

Elmwood Village Office, 715-639-3792.

Wyoming

....

DEVIL'S TOWER NATIONAL MONUMENT

In 1906, President Teddy Roosevelt designated Devil's Tower the nation's first natural monument. But its real claim to fame came from its appearance in the movie *Close Encounters of the Third Kind*. Now it's a UFO seeker's mecca, and one of the most visited geological sites in Wyoming.

The Story:

Located in the northeastern part of the state, **Devil's Tower** rises to the stunning nosebleed height of 865 feet, has a base diameter of one

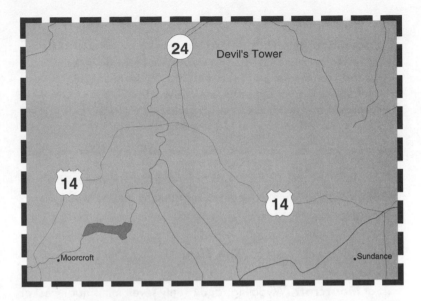

24   Devil's Tower

14

14

Moorcroft   Sundance

thousand feet, and the peak has an area of one-and-a-half acres. The tower's shape might remind you of a giant tree stump. Indian legend says

**Devil's Tower National Monument—
UFO Magnet or Movie Set?**

that it was created by a hungry bear with claws trying to reach Indians who were living on top. But it is actually the core of a volcano exposed after millions of years of erosion brought on by the Belle Fourche River and the weather. You can get to the top only by climbing it or being lowered onto it.

Does Devil's Tower attract alien life? This is the question that many in the UFO community have been asking for a long time, but especially since it appeared in one of history's best known science fic-

ROCKY MOUNTAIN HIGH—REAL HIGH
    The University of Wyoming located in Laramie is the
location for the Rocky Mountain UFO Conference. This
conference draws big names in the world of UFO
research, and is a haven for abductees. Call 800-488-
7801 for conference and lodging information.

tion movies. In the late 1950s, it was rumored that there were several eye-witness accounts of alien craft coming out or going into the tower. Go see for yourself.

The Site:

The monument is open year-round. The entrance is thirty-three miles north-east of **Moorcroft,** Wyoming, and twenty-seven miles northwest of **Sundance,** Wyoming. The visitor center, located three miles from the entrance, is open April through October. Activities are offered from Memorial Day through Labor Day. Parking is limited in summer. Camping and RV facilities are available near the monument.

Puerto Rico

If the number of UFO reports generated by respected ufologists (like Joseph Trainor and George Filer), is any indication, a lot of people in Puerto Rico think they're seeing UFOs. Good thing this is the home of the **Search for Extraterrestrial Intelligence Institute's Project Phoenix**—the basis for the novel and movie *Contact* and the world's most comprehensive search for extraterrestrial intelligence.

The Story:

Project Phoenix is an effort to detect extraterrestrial civilizations by listening for radio signals that are either being sent to us deliberately or inadvertently. Phoenix is the successor to the **NASA-SETI** program that was cancelled by a Congress in 1993 (SETI is now funded privately). Their main administrative headquarters is located in Mountain View, California, and is not open to the public. However, you can visit the famous Puerto Rico observatory where SETI conducts its exciting Project Phoenix work.

If SETI's search ends in success, it will probably be with the help of a radio telescope located in Arecibo, a small town on the north coast of Puerto Rico. This is the big cheese of all the world's radio telescopes—an unrelenting ear pointed permanently into the sky. Visitors to Arecibo are usually stunned by the size of the telescope. It's shaped like a giant birdbath—but for really big birds. It's one thousand feet in diameter. As the site of the world's largest single-dish radio telescope, **the Arecibo Observatory** attracts visitors of all ages and from many countries.

The Site:

The Arecibo Observatory is situated approximately ten miles south of Arecibo in a remote area. The terrain is rough on the feet but soft on the eyes. South of the observatory is the really rugged, hole-in-your-shoes terrain, with jungle, waterfalls, and caves. The hiking is, as they say, out of this world.

Tours are given at the observatory Wednesday through Friday: noon to 4:00 P.M.; Saturday, Sunday, and most holidays: 9:00 A.M. to 4:00 P.M.; schools and special groups (maximum of seventy-five people) can call 787- 878-2612 for an appointment or more information. There is a small admission fee.

UFO/Chupacabra Watching:

Arecibo is where you want to be if you're looking for aliens, Chupacabras, or both. The **Rio Grande de Arecibo Valley** offers some beautiful vistas and an enjoyable ride up Route 10, to Dos Bocas lake. Head there for some serious sky-viewing, but leave the goat cheese behind. You never can tell.

For More Information:
The Puerto Rico Tourism Company, 800-866-STAR.

EL CHUPACABRA

While visiting Arecibo, be aware that according to Jorge Martin, a Puerto Rico-based journalist and UFO researcher, the area around the observatory has been the site of a consistent wave of alleged UFO sightings. There is also a long history of alleged sightings of a frightening creature known as El Chupacabra ("The Goat Sucker"). It is said that this creature lives on blood—not human blood, but the blood of animals (whew!). According to *Outside Magazine* this beast has been wreaking havoc in many areas of Puerto Rico and even Miami for years.

If you visit the many web sites—some hosted by believers, some by debunkers—you will learn that you can draw a few conclusions: Many locals allegedly believe that the creature was either a "pet" of alien races that visited Earth many years ago or is a bizarre hybrid of gray alien combined with a human. Either way, El Chupacabra is not pretty. It's tall, has sharp fangs, and can change its color from green to black or deep brown. Witnesses have described the Chupacabra as a creature with two small arms and clawlike hands. Some say it resembles a lizard that walks on two hind legs. Other reports allege that it has a tail that enables it to fly, or strong legs that allow it to leap hundreds of yards.

Though sightings of it used to be confined to the town of Orocovis in Puerto Rico and to certain areas of South America, the Chupacabra community is apparently spreading (perhaps aided by alien ships), and its population is growing. Sightings of a creature that fits El Chupacabra's description have been reported in Miami, Florida, and other areas.

GLOSSARY
The Lingo of Ufology

Abductees: People who believe they have been physically taken by aliens, either willingly or unwillingly. Abductees typically report having been medically examined or probed in some way.

Close Encounters: famed UFO investigator and founder of the Center for UFO Studies, Dr. J. Allen Hynek, created this classification for close encounters.

Close Encounters of the First Kind (CEOs): The appearance of a UFO within five hundred feet or less of the witness.

Close Encounters of the Second Kind (CE2s): Incidents in which a UFO physically impacts the environment or witnesses. Burned grass or injured witnesses fall into this category.

Close Encounters of the Third Kind (CE3s): An alien being is either observed or abducts a human being.

Contactees: People who believe they can communicate telepathically with aliens.

EBE: Extraterrestrial Biological Entity (basically an alien), sometimes referred to simply as an ET for extraterrestrial.

Flap: A period of intensive UFO sightings. Also referred to as a "wave."

Foo Fighters: During World War II, pilots reported glowing balls of light flying beside their airplanes. These were called "foo fighters," a term based on an expression "where there's foo, there's fire" from Smokey Stover, a then-popular comic strip. The Allies believed that foo fighters were secret German weapons or surveillance devices. Only after the war did they discover that German pilots had also seen the glowing lights, which they thought were secret American or British secret weapons.

Grays: The most commonly reported alien. They are short, gray beings with large, almond-shaped eyes, and large, bulbous heads.

Hot spot: An area with ongoing flaps or frequently occurring flaps.

IFO: A UFO that can be subsequently identified or explained.

UFO: According to the Center for UFO Studies (CUFON), a UFO "is the reported sighting of an object or light seen in the sky or on land, whose appearance, trajectory, actions, motions, lights, and colors do not have a logical, conventional, or natural explanation, and which cannot be explained, not only by the original witness, but by scientists or technical experts who try to make a common- sense identification after examining the evidence."

Project Bluebook: The air force's official investigation of the UFO phenomena from 1947 to 1969.

RESOURCES
Conferences/Meetings/Groups Not Previously Mentioned:

Abduction Support Group-CERO, P.O. Box 131, Verdugo City, CA 91046, Phone: 818-957-3602

Annual International UFO Congress, For information, or to be added to the mailing list, contact: International UFO Congress, 9975 Wadsworth Pkwy, #K2-274, Westminister, CO 80021, Phone: 303-543-9443, Fax: 303-543-8667, Web site: www.padrak.com/ufo

THE MAJOR UFO ORGANIZATIONS:
Mutual UFO Network, Inc. (MUFON)
103 Oldtowne Road
Seguin, Texas 78155-4099 U.S.A.
General Phone: 830-379-9216
To report a UFO: 1-800-UFO-2166
Fax: 210-372-9439
Web site: www.rutgers.edu/~mcgrew/mufon/(This web site
also lists the state directors and has links to state offices.)

National UFO Reporting Center
P.O. Box 45623
University Station
Seattle, WA 98145
Web site: www.nwlink.com/~ufocntr
Center for UFO Studies (CUFOS) Web site: www.cufos.org

TO REPORT A SIGHTING BY PHONE:
UFO Reporting and Information Service: 206-721-5035
MUFON: 830-379-2166
National UFO Reporting Center: 206-722-3000
On-line Resources:
(Also see web sites listed under "The Major UFO Organiza-
tions")

UFOINFO
www.digiserve.com/ufoinfo/
E-mail: Masinaigan@aol.com

Filer's Files
www.digiserve.com/ufoinfo/

Groom Lake Desert Rat
www.ufomind.com/area51/desertrat

Skywatch International
www.skywatch.itlnet.net

The Mothership
www.ufomind.com

Alien City
www.alien-net.com

The Mining Company
www.miningco.com

Alien Abduction Test Site
www.alien-abduction-test.com

The Abduction and UFO Research Association
www.members.tripod.com/~A_U_R_A

Alien Abduction Experience and Research
www.abduct.com

MORE UFO READING:
Above Top Secret: The Worldwide UFO Cover-up.
Timothy Good. 1988. William Morrow & Co.
The Alien Abduction Survival Guide: How to Cope with Your ET
Experience. Michelle Lavigne. 1995. Wild Flower Press.
Alien Harvest: Further Evidence Linking Animal Mutilations
and Human Abductions to Alien Life Forms.
Linda Moulton Howe. 1993. Self-published.
The Allagash Abductions: Undeniable Evidence of Alien
Intervention. Raymond Fowler. 1994. Wild Flower Press.
Area 51: Nightmare in Dreamland. Sean David Morton.
1997. M. Evans & Co.
Casebook on the Men In Black. Jim Keith. 1997.
IllumiNet Press.
The Cash-Landrum Incident. John Schuessler. 1998.
Self-Published.
The Encyclopedia of UFOs. Ronald D. Story, ed. 1980.
Doubleday.
Extraterrestrials. Bill Fawcett, ed. 1997. William Morrow & Co.
The Great UFO Hoax: The Final Solution to the UFO Mystery.
Gregory M. Kannon. 1997. Galde Press.
How to Defend Yourself Against Alien Abduction
by Ann Druffel. 1997. Three Rivers Press
Incident at Exeter/Interrupted Journey. John Fuller. 1996.
Fine Communications.
Intruders: The Incredible Visitations at Copley Woods.
Budd Hopkins. 1987. Random House.
Making Contact: A Serious Handbook for Locating and
Communicating with Extraterrestrials.
Bill Fawcett, ed. 1997. William Morrow & Co.
Mysterious Valley. Christopher O'Brien. 1996.
St. Martin's Press.
Project Bluebook: The Top Secret UFO Findings Revealed.
Brad Steiger, ed. 1995. Ballantine Books.
The Roswell UFO Crash: What They Don't Want You To Know.
Kal K. Korrff. 1997. Prometheus Books.
The UFO Book: Encyclopedia of the Extraterrestrial.
Jerome Clark. 1998. Visible Ink Press.
The UFO Casebook. Kevin D. Randle. 1989. Warner Books.
Unexplained Mysteries of the 20th Century. Janet and Colin
Bord. 1990. NTC/Contemporary Publishing.
Uninvited Guests: A Documented History of UFO Sightings,
Alien Encounters & Coverups. Richard Hall. 1988.
Aurora Press.

UFO
USA

A TRAVELER'S GUIDE TO UFO SIGHTINGS, ABDUCTION SITES, CROP CIRCLES, AND OTHER UNEXPLAINED PHENOMENA

By The Society for the Preservation of Alien
Contact Evidence and Geographic Exploration (SPACEAGE)

HYPERION

NEW YORK

About the Authors
The Society for the Preservation of Alien Contact Evidence and Geographic Exploration (SPACEAGE)

SPACEAGE is a grassroots organization dedicated to preserving the nation's extraterrestrial points of interest and the lessons they can teach future generations. Formed in 1975 by a group of scientists and researchers who claim to have worked at Area 51, the alleged secret military base in Groom Lake, Nevada, SPACEAGE's mission is to research, identify, and promote awareness of sites around the US of interest to the UFO research community, including: sites of alleged spaceship crashes, sites exhibiting physical evidence of extraterrestrial contact, sites of secret military bases, UFO pilgrimage spots, and UFO museums and research facilities. Because of the controversy surrounding many of the sites SPACEAGE identifies as "of significant interest to the quest for evidence of extraterrestrial contact," the members of SPACEAGE prefer to remain anonymous.

The authors wish to thank the International UFO Museum and Research Center in Roswell, New Mexico for their assistance with this book.

Copyright © 1999 Book Soup Publishing, Inc.

A Book Soup Book

A Truly Unique Travel Guide™ is a trademark of Disney Enterprises

All rights reserved. No part of this book may be used or reproduced in any manner whatsoever without the written permission of the Publisher. Printed in the United States of America. For information address: Hyperion, 114 Fifth Avenue, New York, New York 10011.

Photos on page 162 and 171 are Copyright © by Dover Publications.
All other photographs are Copyright © 1999 by Antonio Huneeus.
All maps are Copyright © 1996 by Cartesia Software.
All illustrations are Copyright © 1999 by Book Soup Publishing, Inc.

Library of Congress Cataloging-in-Publication Data
ISBN: 07868-8396-0

FIRST EDITION
10 9 8 7 6 5 4 3 2 1